Messages of
God's Abundance

Also by Corrie ten Boom

Reflections of God's Glory

MEDITATIONS BY THE AUTHOR OF *THE HIDING PLACE*

Messages of God's Abundance

FOREWORD BY CHARLES SWINDOLL

Corrie ten Boom

Zondervan

Grand Rapids, Michigan 49530 USA

Zondervan

Messages of God's Abundance
Copyright © 2002 by Stichting Trans World Radio voor Nederland en België

Requests for information should be addressed to:

Zondervan, *Grand Rapids, Michigan 49530*

Library of Congress Cataloging-in-Publication Data

Ten Boom, Corrie.
    Messages of God's abundance : more meditations by the author of The hiding place / Corrie ten Boom.
        p. cm.
    Sequel to: Reflections of God's glory..
    ISBN 0–310–24570–2 (hardcover)
    1. Christian life–Reformed authors. I. Title.
BV4501.3.T454 2002
242 — dc21   2002006574
                                                   CIP

This edition printed on acid-free paper.

Interior design by Laura Blost

Printed in the United States of America

02 03 04 05 06 /❖ DC/ 10 9 8 7 6 5 4 3 2

Contents

Foreword

by Charles R. Swindoll

Every time I think of it, I'm humbled to the core. I'm both wounded and healed. Injured and restored. I'll tell you the truth, nothing levels me quite like . . . forgiveness.

It happened a short time ago in Israel. I was leading an Insight for Living tour through the painful halls of the *Yad Vashem*, the Holocaust Museum of Remembrance. Each horrifying photograph and caption illustrated in detail the depths of man's sinfulness and also the suffering of individuals and a nation. Dachau. Ravensbrück. Auschwitz. They are no longer words to us—they are wounds.

Stepping outside the dank, gray dimness of the museum and into the warm sunlight provided welcome refreshment. There, lining the path outside the building was the Avenue of the Righteous Gentiles, a lush, tree-lined walkway celebrating individuals who helped rescue Jews from Nazi atrocities. Each tree had a simple plaque at its base, stating the name and country of the honored Gentile. Beside many of the trees were piles of stones, stones of remembrance, put there by people the world over who simply wanted to say "thank-you."

In that bright sunlight, each lost in our own thoughts, we walked the rows of trees. I looked for a friend's name—a woman who has been like a mentor to me in her message of grace and forgiveness. And when I found it, overcome with emotion, I placed a small stone atop the pile. The plaque read: Corrie ten Boom, Holland.

Those of you who know her story as told in her book, *The Hiding Place*, know the message she lived was learned in the schoolroom of suffering. This is always true of forgiveness. It is impossible to experience forgiveness without having endured a measure of pain—the pain of either being offended, or the pain of knowing you have offended someone else. For Corrie, this word of offense was Ravensbrück.

Few had more right to feel bitter than Corrie, yet few have reflected God's forgiveness any greater than she did. How did she do it? How could she forgive those who killed her family, who robbed her of everything?

I thought of this question the following day in Jerusalem. As I stood near the spot where our Savior died, I remembered His words from the cross: "Father, forgive them. . . ."

In the shadow of the cross—with its vertical beam to the sky and its horizontal beam outstretched—I was reminded of forgiveness: both vertical (God's forgiveness of me), and horizontal (my forgiveness of others).

And I knew how Corrie could forgive. She saw it modeled.

I had the privilege of pastoring the church where Corrie attended during her final years. I remember her saying on one occasion that, as children of God, we must be like a mirror, holding up a reflection of God for the world to see. The light doesn't come from us, it's a reflection of His glory. When they see us love, they see a mirror of God in our lives. I'm convinced, especially after standing in that bright sunlight outside the *Yad Vashem*, that nothing reflects God's love and grace greater than when we forgive.

As you know, Corrie's story had only begun when the war ended. Upon her release from Ravensbrück until her death in

1983, she traveled the world encouraging the church and pro-
claiming the Gospel to the lost. Thanks to the ministry of Trans
World Radio, she also became a pioneer of Christian broadcasting. In a wonderful twist of events, her message of grace and
forgiveness beamed across Europe and even into Germany via
the radio transmitters built—but never used—by her enemies to
spread Nazi propaganda! I've visited that infamous building in
Monte Carlo that we often have called "the Hitler building" and
couldn't help but smile at God's wonderful and inscrutable ways.
Who could have guessed in those vicious days of war when that
tower was erected that it would be used to broadcast a message
of healing and forgiveness to the post-war world?

The same is true today. In the United States, as well as around
the world through Insight for Living's partnership with Trans
World Radio, we receive countless letters and messages from
people who tell us how *Insight for Living* has been a mirror of God,
reflecting His provision for their individual needs. We marvel at
God at work. I join with my friends at Trans World Radio in
continuing to pray that, through *Insight for Living* and other broadcasts teaching God's Word, this very personal medium of radio
will give you hope and encouragement, and help you through
the very personal issues of faith and forgiveness.

I was so pleased when my friends at Trans World Radio told
me about these newly found meditations from our friend Corrie
that have never been in print! The first of these "lost writings"
were compiled in the book, *Reflections of God's Glory*, and now continue in this book you hold in your hands, *Messages of God's Abundance*. These are both worthy titles considering the life and
message of this dear saint of God. I smile when I read these pages,
hearing in my memory her rolling Dutch accent and seeing her
wise and clear blue eyes, "Pastor *Svendahl*, do all to the glory of
God."

May you, too, hear her message in these pages and in so doing, give all the glory to God.

Charles R. Swindoll
Chairman of the Board, Insight for Living
July 2002

Acknowledgments

Special thanks to:

Rinse Postuma, director, Trans World Radio voor Nederland en Belgie (Netherlands and Belgium), for special permission to translate and publish the manuscripts in English;

Clara M. van Dijk, retired, Trans World Radio voor Nederland en Belgie, for championing the initial vision for this book and organizing, researching, and editing the original Dutch manuscripts;

Claire L. Rothrock, Trans World Radio—Europe, the Netherlands, for translating all materials from Dutch to English and turning it into a labor of love;

Hans van der Steen, retired director, Trans World Radio voor Nederland en Belgie, for his valuable assistance to this project and for sharing many insights into the life and ministry of Corrie ten Boom gained from his personal relationship with Corrie formed through years of coproducing her radio broadcasts;

Tom Watkins, Trans World Radio—The Americas, for initiating and overseeing this project, and for editing the final manuscript.

Introduction

No matter what the denominational label on our church door might be, by our hearts we are all known by the same name: "The Die-hard Independents!" God says to us, "Your ways are not my ways," and of course we agree—and carry on our own way. "My thoughts are not your thoughts," and our mouths voice their approval—but we never doubt that we know best. Sooner or later, though, if we are truly to build something that lasts for God's kingdom, God must write His words not just on the surface of our lives but down in the depths. It is exactly people like Corrie ten Boom that He uses to do the writing.

Humanly speaking Corrie was weak. No money, few connections, no public relations machine, no fame. All she had was her weakness, a word that doesn't fit easily into our normal vocabulary. It's the opposite of what we call success. Surely to be weak is to fail. It's like . . . well, like a man nailed onto a cross to die. How could *that* possibly achieve anything? All Corrie had was her weakness. Oh, and one other thing: her Lord—crucified, risen, in heaven, and by her side. She simply believed, really believed, that with Him everything was possible, and she passed her days putting that belief into practice. Her weakness became a door through which Jesus stepped to do His all-powerful and perfect will.

Many will know the story of Corrie's life (told in the book and film *The Hiding Place*, and in other books she wrote), how she helped Jews to escape the Nazi regime of World War II, was betrayed by two fellow Dutchmen, and sent eventually, after two imprisonments in Holland, to Ravensbrück concentration camp in Germany. Her experiences were terrible but uniquely equipped her for the post-war role as God's ambassador of love and forgiveness around the world, which became her consuming passion. Men could do their worst, but with a certainty that none could deny or ignore she knew that in the end "Jesus is Victor," the phrase that became her watchword for life.

Corrie's first contact with Trans World Radio was in 1965, and within a year Dutch-speaking listeners in the Netherlands were hearing her radio talks broadcast from the powerful transmitters in Monte Carlo, which TWR has used since 1960. Ironically, it was the Nazis who built these transmitters but never used them; clearly God had other plans! Later her voice was heard by listeners in the Dutch Antilles and in Africa.

But English listeners and readers would never have had access to this storehouse of spiritual treasure had it not been for the tireless efforts of Clara M. van Dijk, now retired from Trans World Radio—Netherlands, who organized these materials and championed the vision for seeing them published, first in Dutch, and now in English. In 1997, TWR staff member Claire Rothrock began her translation of all of Corrie's manuscripts. Twenty-four talks were gathered together and published by Zondervan in 1999 as *Reflections of God's Glory*, and now this second and concluding volume adds a further twenty-six fine meditations to the series. A new generation is discovering to its delight and blessing the warm biblical wisdom that was Corrie's trademark.

Trans World Radio began broadcasting Gospel radio in 1954 and today sends out more than 1,800 hours of programs every week in 180 languages and dialects around the world. By utilizing thirteen super-power transmitters, stretching from the heart of Europe to the Pacific Ocean, as well as by using satellites, the Internet, and more than 1,600 local radio stations and transmitters, TWR is the most far-reaching Gospel broadcaster in the world today. A million and a half responses are received each year from listeners in 160 countries. We praise God for this growth and that many who might never have heard of God's love for them can today hear the Gospel and be strengthened in their faith through radio. And we thank Him too for giving us people like Corrie ten Boom through whom His love speaks so clearly and so powerfully.

Listeners loved Corrie's radio talks, and they were easily the ones that prompted the most letters from Dutch listeners. I suspect this was because people loved *her*. The Spirit of Jesus hung about her in a way that made His love radiate through in almost a tangible way. She has fairly been called one of her generation's most loved women.

From my desk I can see a photograph of the Birkenau concentration camp in Poland, the near neighbor of the more famous Auschwitz. The electrified fence and the watchtowers are still there as necessary reminders of the horror that they once looked down on. But now there is also something else. The parade ground that once held broken, shivering bodies is now carpeted with beautiful wildflowers. Overhanging the fence are the verdant branches of many willow trees, dancing and singing in the breeze. God is steadily taking back that which men had arrogantly tried to claim as theirs alone. It is a picture of life bursting forth out of death, and it is a picture of Corrie ten Boom's life and the lives of those she touched.

There are some Bible verses in which the apostle Paul wrote about Abraham, but they seem to me so applicable to Corrie (forgive me for changing "he" to "she"):

> Yet [she] did not waver through unbelief regarding the promise of God, but was strengthened in [her] faith and gave glory to God, being fully persuaded that God had power to do what he had promised.

Corrie exemplified those words throughout her life. Reading the pages of this book you'll be in the company of a woman of faith whose life gave, and still gives, glory to God. My prayer is that through them God will write deeply in all of us and will change our allegiance once and for all from "The Die-hard Independents" to become those who, like Corrie, give glory to God!

David Tucker, President, Trans World Radio
Cary, North Carolina
August 2002

One

Let Your Light Shine

᙭

In Matthew 5:13 and 14–16 we read that the Lord Jesus says, "You are the salt of the earth," and "You are the light of the world. A city on a hill cannot be hidden. Neither do people light a lamp and put it under a bowl. Instead they put it on its stand, and it gives light to everyone in the house. In the same way, let your light shine before men, that they may see your good deeds and praise your Father in heaven."

I have spoken to prisoners in many countries. During the war I experienced what it means to sit behind a door that can only be opened from the outside. Maybe that is why I am so interested in prisoners and sympathize with them so much. I think of a rough young man in Mexico, who had an eighteen-year sentence. You don't get that for just stealing a car. But something had happened in his life. The Lord Jesus had laid His hand upon him. He prayed, "Come into my heart, Lord Jesus" and Jesus came. That's what it says in Revelation 3:20, "Here I am! I stand at the door and knock. If anyone hears my voice and opens the door, I will come in." And that had happened. The man became an evangelist in his prison. When I arrived there, he had already brought half of his fellow prisoners to the Lord.

I hope that you, the reader, will get to heaven and that I will meet you there. Then I am sure that I'll be able to introduce you to quite a few fervent evangelists whom I met in prisons, fellows who were serving their sentences. But not only that, we will also find many who, through them, found their way to heaven.

I want to tell you something I learned from a prisoner in New Zealand. Sometimes you hear the most wonderful sermons from people who are serving their sentence in prisons. I had preached on the text, "You are the light of the world." Can you say that to prisoners? Wouldn't it be better to say, "You are the darkness of the world"?

One of the men who had heard my sermon said, "This morning I was leafing through the Bible and I found the story of three murderers. One was called Moses, one David, and one Paul." Were they murderers? Yes. We know them as God's heroes, but all three were murderers. The prisoner said: "Mates, there's hope for you and me." What can God do with a murderer who surrenders totally to Him? What can God do with a completely surrendered "decent" sinner like you and me? Will you surrender to Him? Miracles will happen. You will become the light of the world and the salt of the earth.

Let's pray together. "Lord, I thank You that You can use sinners. You didn't call the angels to be evangelists; they have other work to do. But You can use me. Lord, hear those who listen and are saying: 'Can You use me?' Take my life, and let it be consecrated, Lord, to Thee. Oh, Lord, how wonderful it is that You will make them the light of the world and salt of the earth. Hallelujah. Amen."

Two

Two Kinds of Love

ℒ

Because God has poured out his love into our hearts by the Holy Spirit, whom he has given us" (Rom. 5:5). An ocean of love and light covered an ocean of sin and darkness when Jesus said on the cross, "It is finished."

There are two kinds of love: human love and God's love. Human love can fall short; God's love never does. In 1 Corinthians 13 we read about divine love. In the original Bible text there are two different words for love. Human love is called *philia*, God's love is called *agape*. God's love is the greatest reality, here and now—not only if we live in a beautiful house and have enough to eat, but even if the very worst happens in the life of a child of God, the best remains, namely God's love.

I experienced that love when I was imprisoned in a concentration camp during the war. Each morning they held roll call. The supervisor used that time to demonstrate her cruelty. One morning I could hardly bear to see and hear what was happening in front of me. Then a lark started to sing in the air. All the prisoners looked up. I looked up too and listened to the bird, but I looked further and saw heaven. I thought of Psalm 103:11, "For as high as the heavens are above the earth, so great is his love for those who fear him." I suddenly saw that the ocean of God's great love is greater than human cruelty. God sent the lark every day for three weeks to teach us to direct our eyes to Him.

When I was released and went back home, my body carried the scars of the camp for a long time. My friends were afraid that I would say: "The greatest reality in life is human cruelty." But through God's grace I was able to say: "There are three great realities in life. The first is the ocean of God's love in Jesus Christ; second, God's promises; and third, God's commandments."

There is nothing in which God demonstrates His love more clearly than in His promises and His commandments. The amount of God's love is unlimited, but we only receive as much as we use. A tradesman once complained that he was so busy he could hardly bear it. He was a child of God and I said to him, "How wonderful that you don't have to do it alone." "What do you mean?" "Well, what a friend we have in Jesus." "Do you really think that I have time to think of that?"—He looked like a mountain climber who has a guide with him and says to him, "Don't you see how hard it is to climb this mountain? Do you really think I have time for a guide?"

I, too, often get so busy with my work that I have no time to think of Jesus' love. I become impatient and unkind. How much I still have to learn! I cannot gain the victory over life's problems, big or small, by my own strength. When I was in the concentration camp, I sometimes felt hatred rising inside me, but the Holy Spirit taught me a prayer: "Thank You, Lord Jesus, that You have brought God's love into my heart through the Holy Spirit whom You gave me. Thank You, Father, that Your love in me is stronger than all hatred." And I found that there was no longer any room in my heart for hatred.

God wants to conquer our largest and smallest difficulties through His love. Think of the problems in your life at this moment. Are there problems that you cannot conquer with human love? Do it from now on with God's love, God's "agape," which never falls short. "Happy is the man who can draw his love from the heart of his Savior," Count Zinzendorf once said.

A pastor once spoke of God's conquering love in Jesus Christ. A mentally handicapped boy, Toontje, who went to church faithfully but could never understand the sermons, listened this time with great happiness. The pastor forgot the rest of the congregation and spoke only to Toontje, whose face began to beam more and more. He understood something of the ocean of God's love. The next morning the pastor planned to visit Toontje, but he heard that the boy had died in his sleep. There was an expression of heavenly joy on the face of the dead boy. The pastor said: "I believe that Toontje's heart was broken because he tried to grasp too much of God's love." God, who is so great, loves to give great gifts; but oh, we people have such small hearts. But the Holy Spirit continually makes our hearts greater and stronger, until we one day see Jesus face-to-face.

When we are on the beach we only see a small part of the ocean. However, we know that there is much more beyond the horizon. We only see a small part of God's great love, a few jewels of His great riches, but we know that there is much more beyond the horizon. The best is yet to come, when we see Jesus face-to-face.

"Thank You, Lord Jesus, that You poured out God's love in our hearts through the Holy Spirit. Thank You, Father, that Your love conquers today's problems. Hallelujah. Amen."

Three

Working, Inspired by God's Love

I have often spoken about witnessing. We can all be used by the Lord to bring others to Him. That can be quite difficult, and sometimes even very dangerous. In countries where there is no freedom, we may have to die for the Lord. That is not so strange. Even now there are many martyrs who are imprisoned or killed for their witness.

But it is so wonderful that the Lord Himself gives us courage. I remember a story that I heard about a missionary who was going to China. It was still possible then, but it was dangerous. Someone asked her, "Aren't you frightened?" She replied, "No, there's only one fear in my heart. In the Bible it says that a grain of wheat must die to bring forth fruit; now I'm only scared that I'll become like a grain of wheat that isn't prepared to die."

I have to tell you about a boy who worked with me in the underground movement during World War II. His name was Piet Hartog. He was a very brave assistant of mine. I remember that one day we heard that Jewish children in an orphanage in Amsterdam were to be murdered. I called together the boys I worked with and said, "You have to save the children." And they did. My boys got the children out of the orphanage; and my girls distributed them among many families—all in one day. It wasn't very difficult. Just imagine holding a baby in your arms and saying to someone, "Do you want to save this baby? If you don't do it and I can't find anyone else, this baby will be killed." Of course the person will say, "No, no, no, give me the baby."

Piet Hartog said to me that evening, "I believe that we are involved in the most important work there is, saving lives from morning to evening. I don't want to go back to college. This is really essential work. It is wonderful." I said to Piet, "I too am so happy when I think of those babies; but, Piet, do you know that there's even more important work, not only saving lives but souls—showing people the way to Jesus." Then Piet laughed, and said what someone who hears this may say or think: "I am a Christian boy; yes, I'm a Christian. I read my Bible, I pray. I go to church. But telling other people about the Lord Jesus, that's the pastor's job." I said, "Piet, every child of God is called to present the Gospel, and in your life a time will come when you will see that's the most important thing for you!"

Six months later Piet ended up in jail and heard he had only a week to live. The day before he was shot he wrote us a long letter: "All the boys and men in my dormitory are condemned to death just like me. I am so happy that I was able to tell them that if they accept the Lord Jesus as their Savior, He will make them children of God; that a child of God may trust that, if he believes in the Lord Jesus, in the house of the Lord with its many mansions there is one for him. I think it's so wonderful that I could tell them that they only need to tell the Lord of their sins and they will receive forgiveness. The blood of Jesus will cleanse them of their sins. Now I know that presenting the Gospel is the most important thing for every child of God."

I have a message from Piet Hartog for you. Are you a Christian? Don't wait then like Piet Hartog did, to the last week of your life, but say to the Lord today, "Take my life, and let it be consecrated, Lord, to Thee." If you do that, the Lord will use you to tell others about the Gospel. The marvelous thing is not just that we may do it, but that we don't have to do it in our own strength. We only need to tell the Lord and He will do it. We only need to look to the Lord and He makes us, as it were, a mirror of His love. He has such longing and such love for the lost. If we let Him speak through us, then that love enters our hearts. Oh, how wonderful that is. If you do it, and you see people around you later in heaven, some of them will say, "You invited me." If you hear that, you will know that you didn't live in vain.

Let's pray together. "Thank You, Lord, that You want to use us, 'decent' or 'offensive' sinners. If we come to You, You will make us the light of the world. Hallelujah. Amen."

Four

What Do You Reflect?

And we, who with unveiled faces all reflect the Lord's glory, are being transformed into his likeness with ever-increasing glory, which comes from the Lord, who is the Spirit.

—2 CORINTHIANS 3:18

❧

I once had an accident in my hometown. The police helped me and took me away by car. Whenever a policeman in Holland does anything, a report has to be submitted. So out came his notebook and he asked my name. "Corrie ten Boom." He looked up in surprise and asked, "Are you a member of the Ten Boom family we arrested during the war?" "Yes, I am." During that time many good policemen were forced to work for the German Gestapo; they stayed in their positions to help political prisoners. The man said, "I'll never forget that night. I was on duty when the whole Ten Boom family and about forty friends were arrested because they had helped Jews. There was an atmosphere of celebration in our police station rather than a gathering of prisoners likely to die in prison and concentration camps. I often still tell of how your father took out his Bible and read Psalm 91 and then prayed so calmly."

Ten years later the policeman still remembered which psalm my father had read: "He who dwells in the shelter of the Most High will rest in the shadow of the Almighty. I will say of the LORD, 'He is my refuge and my fortress, my God, in whom I trust'" (Ps. 91:1–2).

I like to fantasize about heaven; I know that reality will be a trillion times more beautiful than our wildest dreams. But one thing I know from God's Word, the Bible: we will recognize each other there. Did Jesus say to His disciples on the Mount of Transfiguration, "May I introduce Moses and Elijah?" No, that's not what happened, but the disciples still knew who Moses and Elijah were. Why? Because they had glorified heavenly bodies and in heaven we will know each other far better than we did on earth.

When I see my father again in heaven, I'll ask him: "Do you remember the night we were all together in the Haarlem police station?" He is sure to say, "Yes, I remember that; that was the last night we were together on earth." Then I'll ask him, "Do you remember the policeman who was on duty?" Most likely he will say, "No, I don't recall him." That night Father didn't think, *Now I have to say or do something that will be a blessing to that policeman.* Father was always very relaxed, even in the prison where he died after ten days. Father's whole life was focused on Jesus, and Jesus made him a mirror of His love and His glory.

A mirror doesn't have much to do. To do its job it just must hang or stand in the right direction. You and I don't have to do a great deal either. We need only to look to the Lord Jesus and He will make us like mirrors, and He does it so well! We don't need

to strive and try to be a blessing but just look in the right direction. Then Jesus makes us a mirror of Himself. When you get to
heaven, people may say to you, "You invited me here." Then you
will ask, "When did I tell you about heaven?" You will discover
that Jesus used you when you were really looking to Him.

We are moons, not suns. The moon only reflects the light of
the sun. We need only to reflect light; then we live to His glory.

I looked to Jesus and the dove of peace flew into my heart.
Then I looked at the dove of peace and it flew away. In which
direction are you looking? To your faith? In Hebrews 12:2 we
read, "Let us fix our eyes on Jesus, the author and perfecter of
our faith." Our faith is not the power but the instrument by
which we can use the power of God. I have a small dictating
machine. If it's not working properly, I don't repair it myself. I
send it back to the manufacturer. If my faith isn't working, I
send it back to Jesus, the maker and perfecter of my faith.
When He repairs my faith, it works.

Which way are you looking? To your sins? Oh, turn your
eyes away from your sin and look to Jesus; then you will find
grace. Jesus died for your sins on the cross. He died for you.
He lives for you now. If you have sinned, bring it to Him and
His blood will cleanse you of all sin and unrighteousness that
you confess (see 1 John 1:7–9). In which direction are you
looking? To your concerns? The Bible says, "Do not be anxious
about anything, but in everything, by prayer and petition, with
thanksgiving, present your requests to God. And the peace of
God, which transcends all understanding, will guard your hearts
and your minds in Christ Jesus" (Phil. 4:6–7).

Peter could walk on the waves as long as he looked to Jesus.
But as soon as he looked at the waves, he sank. If you look to
Jesus, the waves in life's storms become like firm ground. Yes,

you and I must look in the right direction: away from our sins, away from our worries, and even away from our faith in Jesus, only to Jesus Himself. Who directs our gaze in the right direction? The Lord Jesus Himself does. Through His Holy Spirit He directs our gaze and makes us mirrors of His peace and His light.

"Hallelujah, what a Savior You are. In You we find solid ground, in which we can sink our anchor forever. Amen."

Five

Who Is Lord of Your Life?

Dear Father, in Jesus' name we pray that You will make things a little clearer about what it means to be ready for the great day that is coming when Jesus Christ, Your dear Son, will come on the clouds of heaven. Thank You for telling us so much about that in Your Word. Help us to understand it better through Your Holy Spirit. Amen.

W hat does everyday life have to do with the second coming of Jesus? Everything, because the Lord could come back today. We don't know the day or hour, but we also don't know a day or hour in which He cannot return. The Lord Himself said that we have to watch for the signs of the times. If we look at world history through the window of the Bible, we know that many signs are apparent in the newspapers. But the wonderful thing is that from God's Word we know that He is interested in us in microscopically tiny things and also in great things. No hair of our head will be lost and God has the universe in His hand. Therefore we need not fear, even if the earth gives way and mountains fall into the heart of the sea. Let us be prepared when the time comes. In what condition will the Lord find us? In what condition will the Lord find you, find me, if He should return today?

I was once visiting a farmer in Australia. He told me that in a nearby village there was a woman of faith who would be wonderful for me to meet. The farmer told me of the many times she had given him advice and how much she knew of the Bible. We had an hour to spare, so we went to visit her. I was expecting a lot in that village, so far away from the city and the rest of the world. I was eager to find this woman who lived close to the Lord.

The hour I spent with her was a disappointment. She talked only of what modern theologians had said, written, and done. She was outraged. She recited all their errors in great detail. At the end of the hour I said, "Well, we haven't had any time to pray together, or to tell something of our own walk with the Lord." We can be led by a spirit of criticism, just focusing on others' wrongs—however unorthodox they may be.

Our hearts can be so ready for battle with those who think differently that it makes us gloomy. Yes, I know we must distinguish between spirits. We are in the days that "false Christs and false prophets will appear and perform great signs and miracles to deceive even the elect—if that were possible" (Matt. 24:24). I am so happy that it says "if that were possible." It is not possible!

We need the Spirit's fruit, yes, and indeed, its gift of discernment of spirits. But that is different from a spirit of criticism, which is always hard-hearted. Led by a spirit of criticism, we set ourselves up to judge fellow Christians who don't think the same way about the inspiration of the Bible, the gifts of the Spirit, or the Millennium. It doesn't help them and it doesn't help us.

Do you have a criticizing spirit? How do handle your money? Are you trying to avoid paying taxes? The ways you use your money are important. How is your marriage? Is it pure? Do you demonstrate love, understanding, tolerance, and forgiveness toward others? You say you can't do it? God can. His love never fails. Romans 5:5 says God's love has been poured into our hearts through His Holy Spirit. Here is the answer again: If there are difficulties, be filled with God's Spirit.

A woman complained of great difficulties in her marriage. Life with her husband was hard, and she was sometimes infected with his darkness. I taught her to pray in her heart, "Thank You, Lord, for Romans 5:5. Thank You, Lord Jesus, that You have brought God's love into my heart through the Holy Spirit. Thank You, Father, that Your love in me conquers my husband's darkness." I met her sometime later, and she said, "My husband has changed completely." Yes, of course he had changed! She had demonstrated God's love to him.

We cannot do it. But He can. We conquer through the blood of the Lamb. You must ask the Lord today, "Is there anything in my life, in my heart, of which I would be ashamed if You returned today?" If the Lord says there is something, repent, because the kingdom of God is at hand.

"No one can serve two masters," the Lord Jesus said at the very beginning of His time on earth. I spoke on this text in a very primitive church in Africa. I felt I wasn't getting my message across. I started walking. The church had a very uneven floor. With my left foot on the high side and my right foot on the low, I walked crookedly down the aisle. It was hard going. When I got back to the pulpit I said: "Did you see how awkwardly I was walking through the church? That's it: serving two masters! It's not easy, and it's very dangerous too." After the sermon, a school principal came to me and said, "I now see that I am walking like a cripple in my marriage, in my personal finances, and with my colleagues at work." He repented of his sin.

Are you walking crippled through life? Keep that up and you will be ashamed when Jesus returns. Give yourself to the Lord and ask Him to fill your entire heart. I once asked an old lady if she wanted Jesus to fill her heart. But she started to tell me that she was very old and very sinful. She could talk of nothing else. I realized then that I had to make things very clear to her. I told how the Lord Jesus says in Revelation 3:20: "Here I am! I stand at the door and knock. If anyone hears my voice and opens the door, I will come in and eat with him, and he with me." I said to the old woman, "Imagine a time when I utterly lack the energy to keep my house clean. I just can't take care of it. Then you come to visit me. When you come in, you see can how dirty everything is. But you also see that I don't have the strength to houseclean, so you say, 'Give me a dust rag and a broom.' And you clean it all up."

The old lady's face began to beam with pleasure when I described such a wonderful role to her. "And then after you have cleaned the house you say, 'I will make a cup of tea and visit with you.' You see, that is what the Lord does. When He comes into our hearts, He sees that they are dirty. He doesn't say, 'I will come back some other time when the house is clean.' No, He cleans it Himself. He purifies us with His blood, and then it is clean. He comes to live in us, He wants to be one with us, and He is host and visitor at the same time." The elderly lady suddenly understood, and with happiness she asked the Lord to come in. The wonderful thing is, Jesus loves us so much, He does it. And He who began a good work in us will carry it on to completion until the day of Christ Jesus.

"Thank You, Lord Jesus, that when You tell us to be pure, You purify us Yourself through Your Spirit. Show us, Lord, if there is anything in our hearts of which we will be ashamed when You return. I praise and thank You, that if we confess our sins, You are faithful and just and will forgive us our sins and that Your blood cleanses us of all sins. Hallelujah, what a Savior.

"Yes, Lord, come quickly, and do what You have promised. Make all things new, so that the earth will be full of the knowledge of the Lord as the waters cover the sea. Prepare me for that great and glorious day when You return. Amen."

Six

When It's Hard to Forgive

S ome time ago I was with a condemned man in his cell. He
was a black man who had been arrested just the day
before and was to die the next day. He was, indeed, executed
the following day. It was during a political uprising in Africa,
and many people were killed. He had been treated roughly. I
could see red welts and wounds. There was nothing in the cell
other than a plank on which we sat side by side. I could see
his handcuffed hands. We had a good conversation, however,
because he, too, was a Christian. He had the hope of heaven.
He had brought his sins to the Lord Jesus, and we could talk
wonderfully about Jesus who loves sinners and who gives us
eternal life.

But then I asked a question: "Can you forgive the men who
brought you here?" "No," he said, "because they are the reason
I am to die." "Yes, I can understand that very well; but I have to
read to you what the Lord Jesus said in the Sermon on the
Mount: 'For if you forgive men when they sin against you, your

heavenly Father will also forgive you. But if you do not forgive men their sins, your Father will not forgive your sins' [Matt. 6:14–15]. The Lord Jesus said that." "Yes, but I can't do it," the condemned man said.

I then told him about an experience I had during World War II in Holland—how a man, whose wife I tried to free from jail, betrayed me. Because of his betrayal, my whole family was jailed and several of them died there. I had hated that man. When I realized I hated the man, I was shocked. The Bible says, in the Sermon on the Mount, that hatred is actually murder. "You have heard that it was said to the people long ago, 'Do not murder, and anyone who murders will be subject to judgment.' But I tell you that anyone who is angry with his brother will be subject to judgment" (Matt. 5:21–22). In verses 44 and 45 it says, "But I tell you: Love your enemies and pray for those who persecute you, that you may be sons of your Father in heaven. He causes his sun to rise on the evil and the good, and sends rain on the righteous and the unrighteous."

When I understood that I hated the man, I brought my hatred to the Lord. Here is the marvelous thing: if we, as children of God, know that we have sinned, then we also know the path to take. We know what we have to do. In 1 John 1:8–9 it says that if we confess our sins, the Lord is faithful and just and He will forgive us our sins and will cleanse us from all unrighteousness that we have confessed. So I did that very quickly. Then the Lord cleansed my heart with His blood, as it says there too. If a heart is cleansed by the blood of Jesus, then He always wants to fill it with His Holy Spirit—and the fruit of the Spirit is love.

In Romans 5:5 it says that the love of God has been poured into our hearts by the Holy Spirit. That love is also love for our enemies, as a fruit of the Holy Spirit. After the war, the Lord used me to bring that man to conversion. He had been sentenced to death because he had caused the death of many people by betraying them. I was able to write to him and tell him that I had forgiven him. That was because of God's love dwelling in my heart. The man then said "Yes" to Jesus before he was executed.

When I told all this to the man now sentenced to death, he saw the light and said, "Oh, but it's true—I can't do it, but Jesus can!" We went to Jesus together, and that man forgave his murderers—because actually they were his murderers. He had not done anything wrong himself, but he had become caught up in politics. I later heard that he sent his wife a message that same day. He wrote, "Forgive the people who brought me here. You can't do it, but Jesus can; and we have to do it because the Lord Jesus taught us to." I was so happy that he had understood. The following day he was killed; but he had been able to write to his wife.

Now I have to ask you something: Can you forgive? Can you forgive the one who stole your husband's or your wife's love? Can you forgive the rival, who through dishonest competition, ran you out of business? Can you forgive the people who slandered your good name? You can't do it; I can't either. But Jesus can. If you forgive your enemies, you will touch the ocean of God's love as never before.

Isn't it wonderful that Jesus is the victor? I have found it more difficult to forgive a friend who has acted as an enemy, than to forgive an outright enemy. Not so long ago, I had forgiven someone, but the feelings kept coming back. I brought it to the Lord again, but it came back yet again. I felt discouraged. Then I learned this excellent image from a friend. We have all heard church bells ring. But in the moment after they have

stopped, you can still hear "ding-dong" and again "ding-dong."
Those "ding-dongs" are like the echoes of anger. The echoes
may continue even when you mean to stop, but if you bring the
"ding-dongs" confidently to the Lord then they will truly be
silenced. Jesus is the conqueror. Shall we thank the Lord for
that?

"Oh, Lord Jesus, how wonderful it is that You don't just tell
us to love our enemies, but, through Your Holy Spirit, You give
us the love that You ask of us. Show us, Lord, if there is a corner
of our heart with a little bitterness—or maybe a lot of bitterness.
We thank You, Lord, that if we bring it to You knowing that it is
a sin, You forgive and cleanse us. Thank You that You fill a
cleansed heart with Your Holy Spirit, and that the fruit of the
Spirit is love—love even for our enemies and for friends who
have behaved as enemies. Thank You, Lord, that You make us
more than conquerors. Hallelujah. Amen."

Seven

Be an "Up-to-date" Soldier

Every child of God has a task in this world. As this world is becoming darker and darker and more disordered, it is good for us to be aware of the task we have received from our Master. He said, "You will be my witnesses in Jerusalem, and in all Judea and Samaria, and to the ends of the earth" (Acts 1:8), and: "You are the salt of the earth . . . the light of the world" (Matt. 5:13–14).

When the Lord gave us such a big plan of action—to the ends of the earth—He first told us how we would be capable of being witnesses: "You will receive power when the Holy Spirit comes on you" (Acts 1:8). Without the Holy Spirit we can't be light, salt, or witnesses. Not in the street where we live nor in the place we work, neither close to home nor far away on the mission field. But we can be powerful through the Holy Spirit, wherever we might be called. The world needs powerful children of light! We have to be up-to-date. The antichrist is marching firmly on with his great army. If the children of light stand idly by, we will be in great danger.

I believe that the kingdom of God is obstructed more by indifferent Christians than by the vigorous marching of the antichrist. A Vietnamese boy once said to me, "Sometimes churches are mousetraps for Christians. They meet there, enjoy the Word and fellowship with the Lord and each other; but they forget that they have been called to spread the Gospel message over the whole world." He is right. There are churches like that. But I am reminded of Oswald Smith's church, a church that is alive, where the people are fed richly, and where they have warm fellowship with each other. I think they have sent out more than three hundred missionaries whom they fully support. No, Oswald Smith's church isn't a mousetrap.

Do you want to join Christ's army? In 2 Timothy 2:3 we read, "Endure hardship with us like a good soldier of Christ Jesus." Do you want to become a soldier in that army? There is an army that is so powerful, so well-armed, and under such perfect leadership that victory is assured. That isn't an army that is fighting for a particular country. It is a world army. Do you know what the future of the world is? A kingdom of peace, of peace on earth equal to that in heaven. An earth filled with the knowledge of the Lord as the waters cover the sea, where swords will be beaten into plowshares. More details can be found in the words of the prophets, the words of the Lord Jesus Himself, and of the apostles, and also in the Revelation of John.

I once heard a story about Napoleon. A new group of soldiers had signed up and he addressed them like this: "Men, if you fight in my army, you can be sure that often when you are hungry there will be no food. In bad weather, you won't always have a roof over your head. You can expect blood and sweat, but I can assure you of one thing; if you fight for me, then you dedicate your life to Napoleon who has never lost a battle.

Think for a minute. If you want to be a soldier in my army, take a step forward." He turned his back to them and waited for a minute. Then he turned back round and looked at the young men. They still stood there shoulder to shoulder. He said, "I'll give you one more chance. Isn't there anyone who dares? I will wait one more minute." "You don't need to," one of them cried, "we all took a step forward." But Napoleon lost his final battle.

King Jesus will never lose. He was a conqueror, He is a conqueror, and He will be a conqueror. He Himself warned us, "I tell you the truth, unless a kernel of wheat falls to the ground and dies, it remains only a single seed. But if it dies, it produces many seeds. The man who loves his life will lose it, while the man who hates his life in this world will keep it for eternal life" (John 12:24–25). Yes, it can mean martyrdom. Peter says in 1 Peter 4:12–14, "Dear friends, do not be surprised at the painful trial you are suffering, as though something strange were happening to you. But rejoice that you participate in the sufferings of Christ, so that you may be overjoyed when his glory is revealed. If you are insulted because of the name of Christ, you are blessed, for the Spirit of glory and of God rests on you."

I was approached by a young man in a country where it was very dangerous to follow Jesus. We had listened with the whole church to what the Holy Spirit had to tell us about following Him who had come from heaven to this earth and had lived here, and then died on the cross at Golgotha because He loved us so much and wanted to save us for eternity.

The young man said, "Now I am prepared to live and die for Jesus if that is what He wants." I read in the young man's eyes the Spirit of glory of which Peter had spoken. The purpose of the global battle in which we find ourselves is "Peace on Earth." John wrote in Revelation 21:3–5, "Now the dwelling of God is with men, and he will live with them. They will be his people, and God himself will be with them and be their God. He will wipe every tear from their eyes. There will be no more death or mourning or crying or pain, for the old order of things has passed away." He who was seated on the throne said, "I am making everything new!"

The marvelous thing about the commission of our Lord Jesus Christ is that not one of His followers needs to be excluded. Every person is either a missionary or a mission field. The Lord Jesus died on the cross for the whole world, and whoever believes in Him will not be lost. But He said more: "Anyone who has faith in me will do what I have been doing. He will do even greater things than these, because I am going to the Father" (John 14:12).

How can that be? You and I doing greater things than Jesus did? Yes. Do you know why? He went to the Father and He is there at the right hand of the Father on the throne of God. He does greater things than He did in the three years that He worked on earth in Palestine, and He wants to do it through you and me. No one is excluded. Maybe you are sick or elderly, or perhaps you can't even go out anymore; but the commission of the Master is for you too! In the service of King Jesus there is no unemployment.

I have seen many old peoples' homes in the world; some were sad, some happy. The happiest and most joyful home I have seen was in the Mike Martin community of Seattle. There were large grounds with various buildings. In one was a boys' school, in another a conference center; and in one of the many other buildings was an old peoples' home. Over one hundred elderly people lived together there. If something happened in the community—for example, Johnny fell down the stairs in the boys' house—the first call was to the doctor, but the second phone call was to the old peoples' home. As soon as the old folks got the message: "Johnny has broken his leg," they started to pray. They prayed for Johnny's healing, for wisdom for the doctor treating him, and for the nurse who would take care of Johnny. The old people participated actively in this way. When they heard I was to visit them for a week, they prayed every day for three weeks for a blessing on the event, and it was exceptionally blessed. There were several missionaries sent by that community and they could count on the continuous prayer of the old people in the home!

Intercessory prayer is never lost. In the book of Revelation, chapter 5 verse 8, it says, "And when he had taken it, the four living creatures and the twenty-four elders fell down before the Lamb. Each one had a harp and they were holding golden bowls full of incense, which are the prayers of the saints." Now you know, just as well as I do, that the atmosphere in an old peoples' home can sometimes be very dejected. There is disappointment and loneliness. But in that old peoples' home in Seattle I saw the happiest elderly people I have ever met. Praying as an intercessor is a blessing to yourself, and that is actually the case with all the work you do in obedience to the Lord Jesus. If you pass on the light to others, then it shines in your own heart too.

Let's pray. "Lord Jesus, forgive us if we have seen and thought so little of the Great Commission—the task of being witnesses throughout the whole world, to the very ends of the earth. Thank You that You forgive us if we bring this negligence to You. You have said that if we confess our sins, You are faithful and just and will cleanse us of all our sins through Your blood. Yes, Lord, cleanse me too of these sins. I thank You that from now on You allow me to work in Your kingdom—each in his small corner and I in mine, wherever You may call us. Thank You. Amen."

Eight

Missionary or Mission Field

༯

Everyone is either a missionary or a mission field. If you have never opened your heart to the Lord Jesus, you are a mission field. I say to you: Reconcile yourself to God. Come to Jesus; bring all your sins to Him. He died for you on the cross and says, "Come to me, all you who are weary and burdened, and I will give you rest" (Matt. 11:28). Jesus will give you rest and answers to your problems now; redemption, deliverance, and eternal life—because you become a child of God. Now a child of God is called to be a light of the world; so listen to what I am going to say to missionaries, because you, too, become a missionary if you say "Yes" to Jesus.

A missionary has in mind the welfare of all he can reach, and in 1 Corinthians 12:7–10 it says, "Now to each one the manifestation of the Spirit is given for the common good. To one there is given through the Spirit the message of wisdom, to another the message of knowledge by means of the same Spirit, to another faith by the same Spirit, to another gifts of healing by that one Spirit, to another miraculous powers, to another prophecy, to another distinguishing between spirits, to another speaking in different kinds of tongues, and to still another the interpretation of tongues." What riches!

Are these meant for you and for me? Yes, of course. Paul says to each one of us in 1 Corinthians 14 that we should eagerly desire the gifts of the Spirit. Yes, that's what a missionary has to do! How important it is for us to reach out for those gifts, as God describes them through Paul in 1 Corinthians 12 and 14. Then we will really experience in practice the rich promises that Jesus gave shortly before He ascended to heaven: "You will receive power when the Holy Spirit comes on you" (Acts 1:8). That power, among other things, consists of the gifts of the Holy Spirit.

But we need to remember that between 1 Corinthians 12 and 14 is also chapter 13. There Paul writes that even if you have all the gifts but not love, you have nothing! In addition to the gifts of the Spirit there is also the fruit of the Spirit. Galatians 5:22 says, "The fruit of the Spirit is love, joy, peace, patience, kindness, goodness, faithfulness, gentleness and self-control." Remember, all these promises are in Jesus: Yes and Amen (see 2 Cor. 1:20). The gifts and the fruit of the Spirit are for you and me. Everything is actually summed up in Romans 5:5, "God has poured out his love into our hearts by the Holy Spirit, whom he has given us."

Some time ago I was in Israel. There was a lot of hatred and fear in people's hearts. One evening a boy came up to me after a service. I had spoken about the ocean of God's love, with which we come into contact through the Lord Jesus and how that love is available to us every day if we give the Holy Spirit room in our hearts. The boy said, "I thank God for today's message. The Lord has taken away all the hatred from my heart.

I can now forgive others completely. I tried before, but I couldn't do it; now I can do it through the Holy Spirit."

I remember speaking to a man in Germany. There was a darkness about him. He approached me after a meeting. Suddenly I recognized him. He was one of the guards in the Ravensbrück camp where my sister died and I suffered terribly. When I saw him, I remembered all the cruelties he had committed. At first, I felt bitterness in my heart. But then something happened. The man told me, "At Christmas I found the Lord Jesus. I brought all my sins to Him and I sought the grace to ask one of my victims for forgiveness. That's why I came. Will you forgive me for all those cruelties?" It was as if a stream of forgiving love surged through me. I was able to shake that man's hand. It was love through the Holy Spirit—because if you forgive your enemies you experience the ocean of God's love as never before.

Let's pray. "Thank You, Father, in the name of Jesus for the tremendous riches that are ready for us, if we just accept them by faith. Thank You that all the promises in the Bible are for us. Thank You that we can fulfill our mission call—not in our own strength, but in Your strength. Give us many opportunities. Will You open closed doors? Will You take all doubt and confidence in ourselves from our hearts, and instead of that give us faith and trust in You, through Your Holy Spirit? Amen."

Nine

A Message of Abundance

Then Jesus went up on a mountainside and sat down with his disciples. The Jewish Passover Feast was near. When Jesus looked up and saw a great crowd coming toward him, he said to Philip, "Where shall we buy bread for these people to eat?" He asked this only to test him, for he already had in mind what he was going to do. Philip answered him, "Eight months' wages would not buy enough bread for each one to have a bite!" Another of his disciples, Andrew, Simon Peter's brother, spoke up, "Here is a boy with five small barley loaves and two small fish, but how far will they go among so many?" Jesus said, "Have the people sit down." There was plenty of grass in that place, and the men sat down, about five thousand of them. Jesus then took the loaves, gave thanks, and distributed to those who were seated as much as they wanted. He did the same with the fish. When they all had had enough to eat, he said to his disciples, "Gather the pieces that are left over. Let nothing be wasted." So they gathered them and filled twelve baskets with the pieces of the five barley loaves left over by those who had eaten. After the people saw the miraculous sign that Jesus did, they began to say: "Surely this is the Prophet who is to come into the world."

—JOHN 6:3–14

I was able to speak twice in an East African prison. People listened very carefully. I felt as those disciples must have felt when they fed those five thousand people—from just five loaves and two fishes. The secret was, they had accepted that meager meal from the hand of the Lord Jesus. A full basket of leftovers remained for each of them. What foolishness, yes, a foolishness of God. In 1 Corinthians 1 and 2 it says that the foolishness of God is wiser than human wisdom. The foolishness of God is the greatest wisdom.

Imagine the disciples attempting this feat with human wisdom. They might have said, "There is far too little for all these people; let's eat it ourselves. We need to keep up our strength, and we don't want to be undernourished." I imagine that those few loaves and fish would have left twelve healthy young men very hungry still. But now, through the foolishness of God, there was a basketful for each disciple! A good meal, after the effort it took to distribute food to five thousand hungry people. Abundance for all. How marvelous.

I experienced the disciples' joy when I saw those men in Africa, with their broken lives, sitting on the ground in front of me. I told them about the ocean of God's love and that there was One who died on the cross out of love for sinners to carry our sin and guilt. I told them what Jesus said: "And surely I am with you always, to the very end of the age" (Matt. 28:20). Our Savior did not only die, but He rose again and lives for us today. I told them: "Among a million others, He also sees each of you. There is One who loves you, who loves you so much that He wants to fill your heart with His Holy Spirit, and the fruit of that Spirit is love, joy, and peace. He says: 'Here I am! I stand at the door and knock. If anyone hears my voice and opens the door, I will come in and eat with him, and he with me' (Rev. 3:20)." Many of the prisoners answered the knock; they opened their hearts to Jesus. He came in, because that is what He said He would do. There was joy among the angels of God (see Luke 15:10).

At the end I asked, "Do you have any questions?" Two prisoners stood up. One asked, "Don't you have a medicine against sin?" I said: "Yes, the blood of Jesus Christ washes away all sins that you confess; and then, when your heart has been cleansed, He will protect you with His blood. In the book of Revelation it says that they overcame by the blood of the Lamb. You can't understand that—neither can I—but it works, and I know that from experience." Then I said to the other prisoner, "What did you want to ask?" He said: "Yesterday you came here, we were hungry and you gave us a lot of food. Today you came again; we were even hungrier, and you gave us even more. But what about tomorrow?"

I discussed the prisoner's question with some African Christians. I asked, "Will you bring these hungry people spiritual food? Many were born again in the past two days, but they are very weak babies in Christ and they need food and care." An African answered, "But we can't do that; we have no car. We must walk; that will take up most of our day." The Lord Jesus said: "I was sick and in prison and you did not look after me"(Matt. 25:43).

That night one of the Africans had a dream. He had a new-born baby in his hands. He looked at it with admiration and love. Then he saw that the baby was about to die, and he was saddened. When he woke he asked, "Lord, what does this dream mean?" The answer was: "That was one of the babies who was born again in prison; it died from lack of food and care." The African called his fellow Christians together and told them his dream. They decided that one of them would visit the prison each Sunday.

May I ask you a question: How far is it from your home to the closest prison? Do I mean that you have to go and work for the prisoners? No. I don't intend it as a criticism. I needed to live behind the walls of three different prisons before I could feel I wasn't too sensitive for such dismal work. So I can understand if you don't dare to do it. But I hope you will read Matthew 25 again; the Lord might want to speak to you through it. This chapter isn't just about prisoners but also about those who are hungry, strangers, and the sick. It can be an eye-opener.

I once received a letter from a German man under a life sentence. He wrote, "Once a month I am allowed to write a letter, but I don't have anyone to write to in the whole world. Could I write to you?" What loneliness. I was deeply moved. Of course I could have replied "Yes." But I am a wanderer, sometimes I travel in countries where post only reaches me very slowly, if at all. I also understood that this man was one of the many lonely people who live behind closed prison doors. I brought the letter before the Lord and He gave me wisdom.

I asked on the radio if there were any people who might write occasionally to prisoners who receive little or no mail. People responded, but they were the prisoners—they so eagerly wanted mail! Oh, that work progressed so wonderfully after the war! If you too want to get involved, write to a prison and ask for an address. It is such a wonderful opportunity to share the love of the Lord Jesus for sinners and show them the way to start a new life. Intercession is very important too, and prayers for wisdom.

Let's pray together now. "Father, in Jesus' name we pray for all the prisoners who are behind closed doors, which can only be opened from the outside. But, Lord, You said in the Bible that You have imprisoned the prison (see Ephesians 4:8 KJV). I know from experience, Lord, that in prison we can be free if we are but united with You. Will You speak to all the prisoners who listen to Christian programs, and say to them: I am here, I live, and I want to be your Friend, your Redeemer. Lord, I know that You will not send away anyone who comes to You.

"Lord, listen too to those who are free but who have suddenly realized that there is work to be done in Your kingdom, and who say: 'Take my life, and let it be consecrated, Lord, to Thee.' If You think it is right and that they need to write to a prisoner, will You tell them? Thank You, Lord, that later on You will say to these people: 'I was in prison and you visited Me.' How wonderful that will be! Make us faithful and resourceful through Your love. Thank You, Lord Jesus. Hallelujah. Amen."

Ten

Are You Living on Petty Cash or a High Bank Balance?

✺

Ionce broke my arm in a car accident. It was very painful. It troubled me that I couldn't bear it. I screamed and cried because it hurt. I was ashamed. I had just finished my book *Marching Orders for the End Battle*. I had written that a child of God has to be strong—and can be strong because the Lord wants to give us what we need. But now I lay there in utter misery and I was weak.

A visitor came and said, "Stop trying to be strong. You just need to stay close to the Lord. He will take care of it." That was liberating. I had tried, but when I stayed close to the Lord and was aware of His presence—the presence of Him who said, "Surely I am with you always, to the very end of the age" (Matt. 28:20)—then I was able to bear the pain.

Sometimes we try to manage on our own resources. Imagine you have a large business and therefore a large bank balance, and a big bill arrives. It would be stupid for you to pick up your wallet to see how much money you had, or if you went to other people and said: "Please check how much money you have with you. How much can we raise together to pay this bill?" No, you would simply write a check and the bill would be paid. It is so wonderful that we may live on the bank balance of the Bible— a bank account that is never frozen.

Every person is either a missionary or a mission field—the people in your office, school, or hospital, and your neighbors. Perhaps you say I have really tried to be a missionary to them, but I couldn't because their doors were closed. I can well imagine that you weren't able to open them, because you can't do that if you are living on your own petty cash. But with the Bible's bank account, we depend upon the foolishness of God, which is much wiser than human wisdom; then we can see that Jesus can enter through closed doors (see John 20:19, 26).

The people around you are in need. They don't know that Jesus died on the cross for the sins of the whole world, including their own sins—and that if they bring their sins to Him, He will wash them away with His blood. We must learn not to depend on the wisdom of the wise, but on the foolishness of God. Then the impossible happens, like the five thousand people in John 6 who had to be fed by the disciples with only a few loaves and fishes. They took it from the hand of Jesus and passed it around—and then, after distributing the food, there were twelve baskets of leftovers!

The Bible's bank balance is extremely high. I am going to mention a few checks: "Who is it that overcomes the world? Only he who believes that Jesus is the Son of God" (1 John 5:5). Another check says: "I will instruct you and teach you in the way you should go; I will counsel you and watch over you" (Ps. 32:8).

Or where Jesus says: "I have come that they may have life, and have it to the full" (John 10:10). The Lord Jesus didn't say, "You will receive power if you do your very best, and then go forth and teach all nations," but He said, "You will receive power when the Holy Spirit comes on you" (Acts 1:8). Then He gave the Great Commission: "You will be my witnesses in Jerusalem, and in all Judea and Samaria, and to the ends of the earth" (Acts 1:8). The Holy Spirit dwelling in us can do it. It says in the Bible: be filled with the Holy Spirit (see Ephesians 5:18).

I have a glove here. It can't do anything, but if I put my hand in it, it can do a lot: writing, sewing, and much more. Now I know of course that it isn't the glove, it's my hand in the glove. You and I are like gloves, and the Holy Spirit is like the hand—it can do a great deal. If I ball my fist in the middle, the glove flops limply. Each finger has to be filled. Therefore, the Bible says, with practicality, "be filled with the Holy Spirit."

When you were converted, the Holy Spirit came into your heart, and God's Spirit witnessed with your spirit that you were a child of God. In Ephesians 1:13 it says, "Having believed, you were marked in him with a seal, the promised Holy Spirit." But it says that those same people from Ephesus needed even more; read Acts 19:1–6. "He . . . asked them, 'Did you receive the Holy Spirit when you believed?' They answered, 'No, we have not even heard that there is a Holy Spirit.' So Paul asked, 'Then what baptism did you receive?' 'John's baptism,' they replied. Paul said, 'John's baptism was a baptism of repentance. He told the people to believe in the one coming after him, that is, in Jesus.' On hearing this, they were baptized into the name of the Lord Jesus. When Paul placed his hands on them, the Holy Spirit came on them, and they spoke in tongues and prophesied."

"Thank You, Lord, that the fullness of the Spirit is for every child of God. Please show me if there is a small part of my life, or perhaps even a big part, that is not open to Your Spirit.

"Thank You that Your Holy Spirit is willing to fill my life to the fullest, just like sunlight fills a room that is open to its light. Listen, Lord, to anyone who says: 'I am throwing the curtains wide open! Fill every corner and make me like a glove that is able to do anything through Your strong hand that fills every finger.' Thank You so much. In Jesus' name, Amen."

Eleven

How Do We Receive God's Gifts?

➳

I once read a book *A Table Full of Gifts* by Annie van Essen-Bosch. Is the book a catalogue of birthday and Christmas gifts? No, she wrote about the riches described in the Bible.

We find in the Bible an abundance of riches, nourishment, peace, happiness, and answers to problems. It is so good to say, "And that is all for you. Come in and sit down and take whatever you want."

The Bible writers were sometimes at a loss in describing all those riches. They used many "un" words. "We have seen unbelievable things," "unfathomable are God's works," "unspeakable joy." When Peter uses these "un" words in 1 Peter 1:4, where he talks about the inheritance that is set aside for us and us for that inheritance, he calls that "an inheritance incorruptible and undefiled" (KJV). What a wonderful assurance—the inheritance kept for us and us for that inheritance.

How come so many words begin with "un"? The promises in the Bible are heavenly promises that we can enjoy now; but we can't describe them with earthly words. "Oh, the depth of the riches of the wisdom and knowledge of God. How unsearchable his judgments and his paths beyond tracing out!" (Rom. 11:33). We must study the Bible and discover how rich we are!

In Möttlingen, Germany, people spoke of the Bible's riches: "Nimmst's, dan hast's" (If you take it, you have it). You need to claim them. When you read a promise it is so good to say, "Thank You, Lord, that is for me!"

That claiming doesn't always happen immediately. Paul, who had so much knowledge and who knew the Lord so well, wrote in Philippians 3:12, "Not that I have already obtained all this, or have already been made perfect, but I press on to take hold of that for which Christ Jesus took hold of me." It is a battle of faith, especially in difficult circumstances, when everything is dark and threatening.

Yet it is possible. I have already mentioned my sister Betsie, who starved to death in a concentration camp. One day, when we had suffered terribly, she said, "What a wonderful day we have had. We have learned so much of the riches that we already have here on earth. And the best is yet to come, in heaven!" She really saw the embroidery of her life from God's perspective:

My life is but a weaving between my God and me,
I do not choose the colors, He works so steadily.
Oft'times He weaves in sorrow, and I in foolish pride,
Forget He sees the upper, and I the underside.

Not til the loom is silent, and the shuttles cease to fly
Will God unroll the canvas, and explain the reason why.
The dark threads are as needful in the Weaver's skillful hand,
As the threads of gold and silver in the pattern He has planned.

We see the back of the embroidery, God sees the front! He knows how beautiful it will be!

Psalm 33:20 and 21 says, "We wait in hope for the LORD; he is our help and our shield. In him our hearts rejoice, for we trust in his holy name." Perhaps you ask: "How can I do that? How can I receive these riches? I don't belong completely to the Lord and I don't understand it either." The Lord Jesus said that you have to be born again. Then you can see the kingdom of God. Being born again is being born into the family of God.

The Lord Jesus gives us new life. He makes you a child of God. On our part, we must and may receive Jesus. Just say "Yes" to the Lord Jesus. Then the Bible will become a table full of gifts!

Paul's jailer asked, "What must I do to be saved?" The answer was "Believe in the Lord Jesus Christ!" (see Acts 16:30−31). Jesus died on the cross for our sins, He became poor to make us rich. Don't overcomplicate things. Come to Jesus and say, "Will you make me, a sinner, a child of God?" If you do that, He does His part.

Let's pray. "Lord Jesus, will You, through Your Holy Spirit, show us our life from Your perspective? In heaven that will be so clear, but we need to know now. Strengthen our faith. I thank You that You do not turn away anyone who comes to You, but that You make them rich children of God. Thank You. Amen."

Twelve

Who Prepares the Table Full of Gifts for Us?

꒾

When I speak about the riches of the Gospel and the wonderful promises in the Bible, I can imagine that some will say, "Oh no, that isn't for me. That's great for my neighbor, who is so pious and the man who is so good, but I am not there yet." Let me tell you about the conditions that the Bible gives us. Jesus said, "Come to me, all you who are weary and burdened, and I will give you rest" (Matt. 11:28).

Are you weary and burdened, bound and not free? Then it is exactly you who can come to Jesus and receive rest and deliverance.

Some time ago I heard Dr. Stanley Jones speak. He was an evangelist who was then eighty-six years old. He had travelled and preached the Gospel in many different countries. It was on the final day of a conference. During the week people were asked to write down any questions—real questions with which they struggled. Dr. Jones laid his hand on the pile of paper. I thought,

"Well, it's going to take a few hours for him to answer all these questions." But something else happened. He said: "All these questions I have read, can be answered with a one-word answer, and that word is 'Jesus.' Yes, Jesus is the answer to all questions and to every need." I thought, "Is it that simple? Isn't he getting off rather lightly?" But then a ray of light entered my heart: He is right! Jesus is the answer!

Whatever the problem, the answer is the same: tell Jesus, tell it all to Him. His name is Wonderful, Counsellor, Mighty God, Eternal Father, Prince of Peace. Tell it all to Him, He is the Counsellor and He counsels!

Are you troubled by your sins? He died on the cross for your sins: read 1 John 1:7 and 9 to see what He wants to do with your sins. He wants to forgive you and cleanse you from all unrighteousness.

Do you feel lonely? He said, "And surely I am with you always, to the very end of the age" (Matt. 28:20). Perhaps you say, "It can't be that simple! Many battles must be fought and many prayers offered, before peace will come at last."

Yes, Paul too said, "I press on to take hold of that for which Christ Jesus took hold of me" (Phil. 3:12). He knew that it was there and that he only needed to take hold of it. The Lord Jesus did not need to press on to it; He had already taken hold of Paul. Therefore Paul could say, "I know whom I have believed, and am convinced that he is able to guard what I have entrusted to him for that day" (2 Tim. 1:12).

Weren't there any people whom Jesus sent away, who He was not able to help? Yes, there were the Pharisees who said, "I am good and even better than many others." If you come to Jesus in your own goodness, then you are sent away, because Jesus accepts sinners. So if you honestly mean it when you say that you are a sinner and that you have sinned, then in Jesus you will find someone who will love you and forgive you and cleanse you. First John 1:9 says, "If we confess our sins, he is faithful and just and will forgive us our sins and purify us from all unrighteousness." Perhaps someone reading says, "Yes, I did that before and experienced that happiness and forgiveness, but my life has grown so cold. When I faithfully read my Bible and had a quiet time, and went to church or to meetings, then I was rich in the Lord. But I have become so unfaithful and disobedient." Go to Jesus with that disobedience. Read Joel 2:25. It says, "I will repay you for the years the locusts have eaten." Here we read that we may return to Jesus with our backsliding and He will give us another chance.

Don't you know how to do that? He is the Good Shepherd and His sheep hear His voice. Read Psalm 23. That is all for you. Talk about it all with the Shepherd. He loves you and understands you so well.

Are you a sheep of the Good Shepherd? Do you know you are, or are you unsure? Go to Him and tell Him. Say, "Lord Jesus, I am not sure if things are right between You and me. Will You forgive my sins and cleanse me with Your blood? I accept You as my personal Savior. Thank You, Father, that I may be Your child. I so much want to have all the riches in the Bible and the wonderful promises." If you do that, He will accept you, because He said, "Whoever comes to me I will never drive away" (John 6:37).

Let's pray. "Thank You, Lord Jesus, that You love us so much that You want to be the answer to our problems. Will You show us through Your Holy Spirit just how rich we can be in You? Will You show us the sins in our lives? We want to confess them to You so that You can cleanse us. Thank You that You love sinners and that You want to change us into victorious children of God. Hallelujah, what riches. Amen."

Thirteen

Do You Long for the Table Full of Gifts?

✣

The Bible is like a table full of gifts. Do you long for these riches? In Psalm 119:20 we read, "My soul is consumed with longing for your laws at all times." If we are consumed with longing for God's gifts, then our life will become a journey of discovery. We are assisted on that journey by the Holy Spirit who is the Owner of those riches. "The Spirit searches all things, even the deep things of God" (1 Cor. 2:10). The Bible also says "No eye has seen, no ear has heard, no mind has conceived what God has prepared for those who love him" (1 Cor. 2:9).

I read these words and said to myself, "Yes, but my love for God is so small." Then I entered and what was on the table? "God has poured out his love into our hearts by the Holy Spirit, whom he has given us" (Rom. 5:5). What abundance! I only had to open my heart and His love filled my heart and gave me love for God and for people. Do you know what I was to experience? God's love was there for deep experiences, for crises as well as for minor events and day-to-day life with the people around me. I can use the highest potential of God's love in everyday experiences. I cannot do it myself, but I don't need to. I can receive, take, get, everything I need. Take it; then you have it!

The same was true when I fought in vain against my sins. I began to analyze myself to find out where things had gone wrong. Then I read: "The Spirit searches all things"(1 Cor. 2:10). It was just like going to a doctor: you don't need to make the diagnosis yourself; the doctor does that. You just tell the doctor what you feel and where the pain is and he will figure it out. The Spirit searches all things in a similar way.

When I am on vacation, I always enjoy looking at menus posted outside restaurants. You can read what is offered and your mouth starts to water as you see all that is available!

The same delight is possible with the Lord's table full of gifts. Yes, it is possible! It is all in the Bible, where we can read all about victorious living. The Bible is God's love letter to us, and it describes the Lord Jesus, who said, "I have come that they may have life, and have it to the full" (John 10:10).

God wants to receive you and me as material in His hands, just as the potter shapes clay. This means that we must make our lives available to Him. This decision has far-reaching consequences, too far-reaching for many of us. We are interested, but it is like being in front of a beautiful shop window. We are just looking and don't intend to pay the price.

We may be pious Christians, but our ego is still on the throne. We love ourselves. The Bible says, however, "But seek first his kingdom and his righteousness, and all these things will be given to you as well" (Matt. 6:33) and "Love the Lord your God with all your heart and with all your soul and with all your mind" (Matt. 22:37). That means losing your life for Jesus' sake (see Matthew 10:39).

Following these commands means surrendering your life to Jesus. He becomes the captain of your ship. You then see everything you possess like the helmsman sees the cargo. The cargo isn't his; he has to deliver it where the owner wants it. That is not a problem, those are the captain's orders.

Our task is to hand over the whole cargo to the Owner. He who gives everything, also asks for everything! In our relationship with God we are so afraid that He will require too much of us. Therefore, we don't stretch out our hands to take. That is because we do not see reality. We need to see, but not like a mirror that reflects what is in front of it, because a mirror does not have any feeling. True sight comes forth out of life, and influences life. It is the Holy Spirit who opens our eyes.

Be filled with God's Spirit! Then you will see what abundance there is, and how safe we can be. It means keeping your life by being willing to lose it.

Let's pray. "Thank You, Lord, that You want everything from us in order to give us everything. Thank You, Holy Spirit, that You open our eyes, so that we can see how rich we are in the Lord. Thank You, Lord Jesus, that You accomplished everything on the cross, and that You became poor to make us so rich. Hallelujah, what a Savior! Amen."

Fourteen

How Can We Get to the Table Full of Gifts?

୬

The Bible describes an abundance of riches: peace that passes all understanding, forgiveness, love, everything in abundance. Why is that for you? Because your heavenly Father knows that you need these things (see Matthew 6:32). God's gifts are not forced upon us: we may receive them with joy and gratitude. God's love does not force anything upon us and it can wait until we stretch out our hands for Him to fill.

We have to be careful that we don't just admire the Bible's promises. We can be just like people standing in front of a beautiful shop window, who don't go in because they aren't willing to pay the price. A price must be paid for the table of riches. Here we see that on our part it is not striving, battling, or trying but a surrender of our lives into the hand of the Lord.

The Lord wants to prepare us for His return. Everything we need is on the table. In 1 Thessalonians 5:23 it says, "May God himself, the God of peace, sanctify you through and through.

May your whole spirit, soul and body be kept blameless at the coming of our Lord Jesus Christ." Is that possible? Yes, because Paul then says, "The one who calls you is faithful and he will do it" (1 Thess. 5:24).

The most important thing for a Christian in these times is to be ready for Jesus' return. The signs of the end of the age are so clearly visible that we can expect Him soon. It gives us courage and comfort to read in the Bible that the Lord Himself wants to prepare us. The bride is being prepared to meet the groom.

In Philippians 1:6, Paul says, "Being confident of this, that he who began a good work in you will carry it on to completion until the day of Christ Jesus." On the cross everything necessary was accomplished.

The Lord expects complete surrender from us. The potter can't shape clay that is not completely in his hands. Complete surrender means making our life available to God. God wants our lives in His hands, like a potter shapes the clay. If we reject God's desire as too extreme, then we are just "interested," like the window-shopper who doesn't want to pay the price. Our interest soon passes away.

No person is complete by himself. Something has to be added to make life worth living. We are all looking for that "something." There is an emptiness to be filled. We often accept less than top-quality filling. We must seek truly great content so that all parts of our being are filled.

The Lord Jesus says, "I have come that they may have life, and have it to the full" (John 10:10). With these words Jesus provides an answer to our need. He offers us a life of abundance. He wants to enter into a covenant with you. That demands complete commitment from both parties.

The result is a new person—you in the Lord, He in you. Then we can rejoice in our redemption, because we no longer stand there as sinners. Because "God made him who had no sin to be sin for us, so that in him we might become the righteousness of God" (2 Cor. 5:21). We become a new creation.

Often the "old being" still wants to have its say. In Ephesians 6 it says that we need the armor of God. We need that to the very end. But we are standing on victory ground!

Are you worrying about your sins? We need to discern who is showing us our sins. The devil is an accuser of the children of God. He has a full-time job. Day and night he comes with his reproaches. When he has the chance, the accuser says, "There is no hope for you; you aren't good enough." But when the Holy Spirit shows us our sins, it is always in the light of the finished work of the cross. He says to us, "Jesus died on the cross for the sins which now weigh so heavily upon you." The prophet Isaiah says, "But he was pierced for our transgressions, he was crushed for our iniquities; the punishment that brought us peace was upon him" (Isa. 53:5).

Read Romans 8:31–34: "What, then, shall we say in response to this? If God is for us, who can be against us? He who did not spare his own Son, but gave him up for us all—how will he not also, along with him, graciously give us all things? Who will bring any charge against those whom God has chosen? It is God who justifies. Who is he that condemns? Christ Jesus, who died—more than that, who was raised to life—is at the right hand of God and is also interceding for us." For children of God worried about their sins, a table full of gifts is described there.

What exactly is surrender? We know that we may not compromise. It is not a question of feeling but of the will. In her book, *A Table Full of Gifts*, Annie van Essen-Bosch writes of how we can only really receive God's gifts if we bring our sins and problems to the Lord. Then there is room for what God wants to give us. If pride, resentment, hard-heartedness, and all our burdens are brought to the Lord, indeed our whole life, then He can richly give that life back to us. Then we are no longer owners, but stewards. We can feel so rich and joyful if we give Him, the Creator, the ownership of our life.

I saw such a good example of surrender in my father. He sometimes said, "My name is on my watchmaker's shop but actually God's name should be on it. Because I am a watchmaker by the grace of God." He knew what surrender meant, and how we can be stewards.

Let's pray. "Lord, will You prepare us for Your return? I give myself completely to You, so that You, who began a good work in me, may carry it on to completion until the day of Christ Jesus. Hallelujah. Amen."

Fifteen

A New Creation

Therefore, if anyone is in Christ, he is a new creation.
—2 CORINTHIANS 5:17

꒰

I f we meet the Lord Jesus, it isn't a question of half measures.
We don't get anywhere by patching things up; that's unnec-
essary. When He renews and redeems us, it isn't like a flag that
flies on a ramshackle house. It is a completely new house. The
Lord Jesus gives us the right to be children of God, a new
creation, sanctified and holy.

You may say, "Wait a minute; it can't happen just like that.
Aren't we inclined toward evil, unable to do anything good?"
That's true. But Christ makes us a new creation! It is very
healthy and necessary to be aware of your sins, to discover
them. But it is one of the devil's tricks that he makes us think
that it is particularly pious if we go about weighed down deeply
by our sins. The awareness of sin is a needed, transitory phase
in your spiritual life. The devil tries to make it the center—a

pitfall with steep sides. Yes, our sins may be many, but on the cross everything necessary to redeem us was accomplished.

There is life and salvation in looking to the cross. If we look to the Lord Jesus we forget everything else. The wonderful appearance of His being is the hour of the birth of our new self. Our new eyes must start to see other things. Our new heart has to beat and it has a different rhythm!

Paul calls us saints and the family of God, and as if that weren't enough, a temple of the Holy Spirit. You may say, "That's possible for a mature Christian, a child of God beyond reproach. Yes, they can be temples of God's Spirit. But me . . . ?"

Let's see what the Bible says in Isaiah 57:15: "For this is what the high and lofty One says—he who lives forever, whose name is holy: I live in a high and holy place, but also with him who is contrite and lowly in spirit, to revive the spirit of the lowly and to revive the heart of the contrite." John says, "If anyone acknowledges that Jesus is the Son of God, God lives in him and he in God" (1 John 4:15). In Revelation 3:20 we read that the Lord Jesus Himself takes the initiative: "Here I am! I stand at the door and knock. If anyone hears my voice and opens the door, I will come in and eat with him, and he with me." He is going to dwell within us and we can be sure that He will hold a great spring cleaning. He makes us new people, a new creation. Perhaps you say, "But is it really that simple?" Yes, it is very drastic, but also very simple.

I once visited a prison in Germany. I spoke to a man in his cell and he came to the Lord through the text Revelation 3:20. The pastor came in later and I said, "Tell the pastor what happened." The man started out on a long story about a spiritual discussion with me, a new vision, and a long, complicated tale. I interrupted him and said, "Stop. Just tell him what happened. Someone knocked. Who was that?" He immediately said: "Jesus." "Some-one opened. Who was that?" "Me." Suddenly he saw how simple it was and how real. The next day I heard him give a clear testimony during a meeting full of ex-prisoners.

Did you hear it? Someone is knocking. Who is that person? Jesus. Someone has to open the door; who is that person? You. Will you do it?

"Thank You, Lord Jesus, that You came in and made me a new creation. Thank You for the big spring cleaning, for Your blood that cleanses us from all sin. Thank You that You will now really come and live in the heart of anyone who says, 'Jesus knocked. I said "Yes,"' and that You make them a new person, a new creation. Hallelujah. Amen."

Sixteen

Have You Been Born Again?

⤳

The Lord Jesus once said, "You should not be surprised at my saying, 'You must be born again'" (John 3:7).

The question I am going to ask you is, have you been born again? You may read these meditations regularly; you may perhaps read your Bible, go to church, and pray. But have you been born again?

In Revelation 3 you can read about people in Laodicea who were quite religious. If you were to ask them, "How are things going for you spiritually?" they would say: "We are rich, very rich, and we have no need of anything." But there was something very important missing. The Lord Jesus stood outside the door of their hearts and He was knocking on their hearts. He said: "If anyone hears my voice and opens the door, I will come in and eat with him, and he with me" (Rev. 3:20).

You see, if you have not yet been made completely new, then really the answer is to be born again. Is it that simple? Yes. If Jesus comes into your heart He will perform that miracle. You will be born into the family of God. Jesus said, "You should not be surprised at my saying, 'You must be born again.'"(John 3:7). It is the obligatory way, the way you must go. Of course, Jesus performs the miracle of rebirth, but you have to come—you must come. Is that what you want? If so, what do you have to do? Jesus is knocking and you have to let Him in now. What happens when Jesus comes into your heart? He sees your sins; and you suddenly see them very clearly too. There is no other way.

The wonderful thing is that you now know what you must do about your sins—confess them. "If we confess our sins, he is faithful and just and will forgive us our sins and purify us from all unrighteousness" (1 John 1:9). The blood of Jesus cleanses us. Jesus starts working in your heart. He washes away the sins you confess. Is that all as far as sins are concerned? No, it isn't just confessing them, it is also turning away from them. But you are no longer on your own. Together with Jesus you wage war against sin.

You cannot do it alone, but He can do it. He puts the Holy Spirit in your heart and that brings the fruit of the Spirit (see Galatians 5:22): love, joy, peace, patience, kindness. . . . The Bible suddenly becomes very different; it becomes a love letter from God. If you ask Jesus to come into your heart, then He comes and His Spirit confesses with your spirit that you are a child of God. You start to understand the Bible and it makes you extremely joyful, because you see the answer to your problems, the biggest problems in your life.

Everyone has at least two big problems: the problem of sin and the problem of death, and they are answered. You see, Jesus carried the sin of the whole world on the cross, including your sins. He accomplished everything there. He suffered terribly, He was in awful pain, but He wanted to do that out of love, to pay for our sins.

We are also strengthened in our struggle against sin. You are redeemed and you are also victorious over your sins in Jesus. Coming to Jesus is just a beginning. The birth of a child is a start, and being born again is also a beginning. It is the start of a life glorifying God—a victorious life, a life strong through the redemption, help, and presence of the Lord Jesus.

Have you not been born again? Come to Jesus then! What do you have to do? Speak to Him, very simply. He has knocked on the door of your heart and you heard it today; and now He is waiting. The Lord Jesus is gentle; He doesn't force down the door of your heart. You have to open it, and if you really mean it when you say, "Yes, Lord Jesus," then He will come in. In John 1:12 it says, "Yet to all who received him, to those who believed in his name, he gave the right to become children of God." Then you are a child of God. Will you let Him in?

Let's pray. "Lord Jesus, will You make the way clear for him, for her, who is now making a decision for You. Will You remove all resistance, all doubt, all 'yes, buts' and also all the devils and demons because they don't want them to do it; but I thank You that You will send those demons away. Make the path clear between You and him or her. Thank You, Lord. Thank You."

Now we will be quiet for a moment, and you can give your answer to the Lord.

"Thank You, that he or she can now say: 'Yes, Lord Jesus, come into my heart, make me a child of God, perform that great miracle in me of being born again into Your family.' Thank You, Lord Jesus. Amen."

Now you must speak to the Lord some more. You belong to Him. He hears everything you say and He loves you so very much!

Seventeen

A Very Important Decision

≫

There was once a jailer in a prison in Philippi who asked a question you, too, along with many other people, might share. He asked Paul (Acts 16:30–31), "Sirs, what must I do to be saved?" Paul answered with a very short sentence: "Believe in the Lord Jesus, and you will be saved—you and your household." Is it really that simple?

I remember a conversation I had with a doctor in New Zealand. I had spoken to him for a whole day about conversion and what he had to do, but he didn't want to make a decision for the Lord Jesus. There came a moment when I said to him, "Accept Jesus, believe and trust in Him and you will be saved." He was suddenly able to do it and he said, "Yes, Lord Jesus, I believe in You. Thank You for rescuing me and that I am now saved." Do you know what I wondered when he said that so simply? "Is it really so simple and easy?" Yes, it is that easy; it is that simple. That is to say, it wasn't at all easy for the Lord Jesus to make it possible. It was a terrible, heavy cross that He had to bear, and on which He died after suffering terribly. But He did everything necessary for us to be saved.

Now, on our part, we need to stretch out our hands. You see, if I want to give you something you have to stretch out your hand so that I can put it in it. It is just like that with salvation. You have to stretch out your hands and then Jesus lays salvation in them. It is saying "Yes" to Jesus. Nothing else? Well yes, there is more, but that will come later. The big decision, that "Yes," is the most important.

I once asked a woman: "Would you like to accept the Lord Jesus?" She responded, "Oh, I have prayed so much in my life, and the Lord heard my prayers and I know that He blessed me so much. He helped me when life was terribly difficult." Then I said to her: "Look, if a boy asks a girl to marry him and she says: 'You have helped me so much, you have been so kind to me, we have had such good conversations, I am so happy that you have always been so good to me,' then the boy would say, 'Yes, that is all well and good, but we aren't talking about that now. I want you to say "Yes" because I love you.' All being well, she won't think of all that has happened, but she will say 'Yes!' That short, decisive word means great joy for them both, but it is just the beginning."

You may have already experienced much with the Lord. You already love Him, and you know that He loves you. You have prayed a lot, and many prayers have been answered, but the Lord Jesus loves you so much that He is not satisfied with anything less than having your heart, your love. If you say: "Yes, Lord Jesus, I accept Your salvation, I want to belong to You," then He will save you for all eternity. Then you belong together, Jesus and you. That is a wonderful start, just as a "Yes" from a girl to a boy is also a beginning. This, however, is much bigger, because Jesus gives you eternal life. He gives you an answer to the problem of your sin. He makes you a member of God's family. The Bible becomes a love letter from God to you—all because you have now accepted Jesus. He will fill your heart with His Holy Spirit and its fruit—love, joy, peace, and much more. Will you say "Yes" to Him? Don't look at everything you have already experienced—either difficult or wonderful. Simply realize that Jesus is here. He loves you and He wants to take you in His arms. He wants to make you happy and give you eternal life. He wants to give you a victorious life now, He wants to give you His Spirit. He has asked you. What is your answer?

Let's pray. "Lord Jesus, I thank You that You love her and love him so much. Thank You for being so happy when he or she says 'Yes,' and that You will then save them. Did You hear who said this, Lord? Yes, of course You heard whoever said: 'Yes, Jesus.' You didn't just hear it, but You are happy about it. Lord, did You see the people, did You see that one there, who really wanted to do it, but didn't? You know why. There was a 'Yes, but' and that is the very opposite of 'Yes.' Oh, Lord Jesus, will You take away the 'Yes, but'? Will You take away the whispering of the enemy who says that it can't be that quick, that it isn't that easy. Make the way free between Yourself and him or her.

"Thank You that the path is now free of obstacles. Lord, You have heard him or her who also said: 'Yes, Jesus, I mean it.' Thank You, Jesus, that You now lay Your hand on their lives and that You will bring her and him in, and that You have saved them. Thank You, Lord Jesus. What love! Hallelujah. Amen."

Eighteen

In Black and White

For if you forgive men when they sin against you, your heavenly Father will also forgive you. But if you do not forgive men their sins, your Father will not forgive your sins.

—MATTHEW 6:14–15

We read the signs of Jesus' return in both the Bible and the newspapers. The Bible says in Mark 13:35 and 1 John 3:3, "Therefore keep watch" and "Everyone who has this hope in him purifies himself, just as he is pure." Well, the signs are clear. The continual rumors of war, people consumed with fear and anxiety about the world's future, Israel back in its own country, increasing persecution of Jews and Christians, and the rise in spiritism.

Let's consider this: if Jesus were to return today, would you be ready? Are you one of the wise or foolish virgins in the parable in Matthew 25:1–13? Are you a bride with a heart full of love for the Bridegroom and full of longing for His return?

Paul warns us so clearly in 2 Corinthians 5:20, "We are therefore Christ's ambassadors, as though God were making his appeal through us. We implore you on Christ's behalf: Be reconciled to God." You are not reconciled to God if you are unreconciled with your fellow human beings. I once had a disagreement with some Christian colleagues. They did something unpleasant toward me. I was angry, but I brought it to the Lord. He forgave my anger, cleansed my heart with His blood, and I forgave them. Or so I thought.

Then a good friend told me, "Your friends aren't at all concerned about what happened. They simply say that they didn't do it." I replied, "That's easy for them to say, but I have it in black and white." "Oh," my friend answered, "in black and white? Tell me, where are your past sins? You, yourself, told me that they have been thrown into the depths of the sea, and there is a sign: 'No fishing.' As far as the west is from the east so far has he removed our transgressions from us. The Lord even says in Isaiah 44:22, 'I have swept away your offenses like a cloud, your sins like the morning mist.' Your sins are gone, but you still have their sins in black and white?"

I was shocked. I collected all the letters from these friends and burned them. It was a sweet fragrance to the Lord. I felt so happy. The Lord Jesus says in His warning in Luke 21:36, "Be always on the watch, and pray that you may be able to escape all that is about to happen, and that you may be able to stand before the Son of Man." I know that neither you nor I will be able to do that if we still keep the sins of others in black and white. Jesus could very well return today. Don't go to sleep before all that black and white is burned.

In his book *Sit Walk Stand*, Watchman Nee explains very clearly how it is really possible for a child of God to forgive once you realize who you are in Christ Jesus. When the Lord died on the cross, He did not just carry your sins away but also your old self was crucified with Him. And so the unforgiving you, who finds it impossible to forgive, has been crucified and completely taken away.

God dealt with the whole situation on the cross; there is nothing left for you to settle. Just say to Him, "Lord, I cannot forgive and I will no longer try to do it; but I trust that You in me will do it. I can't forgive and love, but I trust that You will forgive and love in my place and that You will do these things in me." God is so rich that it is His greatest joy to forgive. His treasure stores are so full that it grieves Him when we refuse to allow Him to richly lavish these treasures upon us.

Paul says in Colossians 3:12–15, "Therefore, as God's chosen people, holy and dearly loved, clothe yourselves with compassion, kindness, humility, gentleness and patience. Bear with each other and forgive whatever grievances you may have against one another. Forgive as the Lord forgave you. And over all these virtues put on love, which binds them all together in perfect unity. Let the peace of Christ rule in your hearts, since as members of one body you were called to peace. And be thankful." This text is a diving board. We need to plunge into the ocean of God's love. We must take a running jump, a deep dive, into that ocean, throwing ourselves into the lake of His love. Have you taken a running jump today?

In Romans 5:5 it says that the love of God has been poured out into our hearts by the Holy Spirit who has been given to us. If you throw an open bottle into the sea, it immediately fills with water. So, too, by complete surrender into the hands of our Savior, we are filled and surrounded by the ocean of God's love. Just what we need and so overwhelmingly wonderful! "If

I speak in the tongues of men and of angels, but have not love. ... If I have the gift of prophecy and can fathom all mysteries and all knowledge, and if I have faith that can move mountains, but have not love, I am nothing" (1 Cor. 13:1–2).

Have you ever doubted your love for the Lord and your love for your enemies? I did. Have you ever doubted the love of God for His Son Jesus? Never, never. Do you know that Jesus welcomes you in that love? Take the plunge!

"May God himself, the God of peace, sanctify you through and through. May your whole spirit, soul and body be kept blameless at the coming of our Lord Jesus Christ. The one who calls you is faithful and he will do it" (1 Thess. 5:23–24).

"Lord Jesus, show us all where we have kept records in black and white of other people's sins. Our love, our power, is too small; but Your love and power wants to burn the accounts today. In that way You are preparing us for Your return. Thank You that You who began a good work in us will carry it on to completion until Your day, the day of Your return. Hallelujah. Amen."

Nineteen

A Few Thoughts on Guidance

〜

W e were sitting with a group of boys and girls around a campfire. The campers had asked me to talk about my travels around the world.

I told them how the Lord had said, "Go to Japan." I had arrived in Japan, not knowing a single word of Japanese. I, nevertheless, obeyed and the Lord opened many doors for me. I was able to work in the largest prisons in Japan.

A boy interrupted me: "I don't get that at all, when you say 'the Lord said.' Explain HOW the Lord said that. Did you hear a voice, or did you sense something in your thoughts, or in your heart? You said yesterday that it was important to know the will of God. I don't want to argue with you, but I really want to know. What does God want and how does He show us His will? I can't figure it out. How do you do know?"

"Thank you for this question. We all struggle with it, sooner or later, as we seek to walk with the Lord. I believe it is one of the most important things in our lives as Christians. Knowing the will of God should be the number one prayer request both for yourself and in your intercessions for others. You often arrive at a crossroads in life, and you must know which path to take. You feel so safe if someone who knows the way will be your guide."

First, we need to find out what the Bible says about guidance. I remember the Bible text my mother and father were given on the occasion of their marriage. It hung in our living room when I was young. "I will instruct you and teach you in the way you should go; I will counsel you and watch over you" (Ps. 32:8). John writes, "We know also that the Son of God has come and has given us understanding, so that we may know him who is true. And we are in him who is true—even in his Son Jesus Christ. He is the true God and eternal life" (1 John 5:20). Jesus Himself said, "But when he, the Spirit of truth, comes, he will guide you into all truth" (John16:13).

No one gets lost on a straight path. All the promises in the Bible are in Jesus: Yes and Amen (see 2 Corinthians 1:20). That means that they are there for you and for me—whether you have known the Lord for a long time, or only accepted the Lord Jesus today or have yet to accept Him as Savior and Lord. You see, it is just a beginning.

All the riches described in the Bible are your possession. It is a like a checkbook. The checks are in your name and have been signed by Jesus. Now you have to cash the checks. The devil says that the Bible's bank account has been frozen, but that is a lie. That is why you must read the Bible as a love letter from God. For every promise you read, say: "Thank You." Say "Thank You," too, for the promise of Psalm 32:8, "I will instruct you and teach you in the way you should go; I will counsel you and watch over you."

One of the most important tasks is to know God's will. We Christians are often much too busy with unimportant things. If you do not know the will of the Lord, you must put everything aside and concentrate on finding out which path is right. There was once a country with a port that was very dangerous. Under the surface of the water there were many rocks. Now there were clear markers, but you couldn't see them at night. So the people set up six beacons, three on the left and three on the right. If the lights formed two straight lines, then the helmsman knew that his course was safe. God gives His guidance in three ways. If these three are in agreement, then you know that you are safe:

1. Prayer
2. God's Word, the Bible
3. Circumstances

If you know God's hidden companionship, your prayer will become a conversation instead of a soliloquy. Here is an exercise that you could call keeping "my eyes . . . ever on the LORD, for only he will release my feet from the snare" (Ps. 25:15). You learn to recognize God's voice. Job says, "Submit to God and be at peace with him" (Job 22:21). But verse 22 is also true: "Accept instruction from his mouth and lay up his words in your heart." You have to be prepared to obey Him.

Just after the war, I had a very clear experience. I said, "I will work wherever God leads me, but the one country I never want to go to is Germany." After that when I asked for guidance, I received absolutely none. I didn't know what was wrong, but I understood that there must be disobedience somewhere. You see, it is so good to go to the Boss immediately to consult Him. I asked the Lord, "Is there disobedience somewhere?" The answer came immediately: "Germany." "Then I will go to Germany too," I replied and contact was restored.

In my books you may read that the Lord used me more in Germany than in any other country. The German people aren't my enemies. My greatest friends live there, but there had been enemies too. Even the fact of those former enemies became a wonderful experience. When Jesus tells you to love your enemies, He gives you the love that He asks of you.

Make a game of asking for God's guidance so you will practice it:

- ask for it;
- really want it, long for it;
- if you get it, accept it.

As you seek God's guidance you discover that God takes the initiative in your life. He will redirect you if you start out on the wrong path. The Good Shepherd finds it so important that you do His will, that if one sheep strays, He will willingly leave ninety-nine at home and look for the lost one.

The first step is to ask Jesus to be your Lord. If you go on a train journey, you first find out which train you need to take. If you are on the right train, you don't need to worry about red and green lights; the engineer takes care of that. If you need to change trains, the conductor tells you when. The Lord Jesus is the engineer. Place your trust in Him. The Holy Spirit is the conductor; obey His leading! You will know whether you are being guided by Him, because, when you are, you experience peace that passes all understanding. The enemy can imitate a lot, but not God's peace. To receive God's peace, you have to be at peace with Him and that is possible if you open your heart to Jesus. "Here I am! I stand at the door and knock. If anyone hears my voice and opens the door, I will come in and eat with him, and he with me" (Rev. 3:20).

"Thank You Lord, for being such a good Shepherd. Thank You that You lead Your sheep safely. I place my hand in Yours and together—You and I—we push onwards. What a safe way that is. Amen."

Twenty

Jesus, the Messiah

⁊

Today I want to speak to Jews and those who love them, for they can then pass on this message.

In 1844 there was a watchmaker in Haarlem who received a visit from Pastor Witteveen. They discussed the needs of Jerusalem and they both decided to start a weekly prayer meeting in their respective neighborhoods where Christians could pray for the peace of Jerusalem and blessings for the Jews. My grandfather (for he was that watchmaker!) started that prayer meeting in his watchmaker's workshop. The prayer meeting was so remarkable in that period that my father, who told me about it, knew the year it had started. Christians now frequently pray for Jews, but it was not so common then.

A hundred years later my grandfather's son and many grandchildren were arrested in that same house, because they had saved Jews. The majority of them died in prison. Such was the incomprehensible but divine answer to my grandfather's prayers. During the German occupation from 1940–1945, we did everything we could to save Jews from Adolf Hitler's terrible plans. Friends often warned us. They said, especially to our father, "You will end up in jail if you always have Jews in the house. Stop that dangerous work." Father then answered, "I am too old for life in prison, but it will be an honor to give my life for God's holy people, Israel." He spoke truly. Ten days after Father was taken to Scheveningen jail, he died.

Jesus, the Messiah, will return again. One of the most obvious signs of the Messiah's imminent return is the return of the Jews to their country (see Isaiah 66:8, 20, 22). One of the most important moments in the history of our times was May 10, 1948. Rees Howells, who had great love for the people of Israel for whom he seriously and faithfully prayed, said, "The rebirth of the state of Israel is the greatest act of God in 2000 years." God is working in the hearts of present-day Jews to prepare them for the Messiah's return. A rabbi who studied Isaiah seriously and with faith came to the conclusion that two Messiahs must come, the suffering servant of the Lord of Isaiah 53 (Ben Joseph), the other one the coming King of Isaiah 66 (Ben David). We, who have both the Old and New Testaments, know that there is only one Messiah: Jesus, who first came as a suffering servant of the Lord, who bore the sins of the whole world when He died on the cross, and who will return as the King of Kings. Every knee shall bow to Him (Phil. 2:10) and every tongue shall confess Him. Then He will bring about the kingdom of God on this earth, and the prayer that has been prayed by so many millions in the Lord's Prayer, "Your will be done on earth as it is in heaven," will be answered.

The Jews are God's ancient people. They too shall see Jesus. The prophet has already said, "They will look on me, the one they have pierced" (Zech. 12:10). There is no political answer to the needs of this age. The scholars claim that there is no hope, that the world can perhaps exist for another thirty years, but then the end will come. The greatest and most wonderful answer is that the Messiah will return and make all things new. Then the earth will be full of the knowledge of the Lord as the waters cover the sea. Right now the earth is full of crime, pollution, hatred, and disasters. But there is hope; there is a future for the world. The best is yet to come! Whenever you see the great needs of the world, pray: Come, Lord Jesus, come quickly. "The Spirit and the bride say, 'Come!' And let him who hears say, 'Come!' Whoever is thirsty, let him come; and whoever wishes, let him take the free gift of the water of life" (Rev. 22:17).

The Lord in heaven is not surprised at what is happening now. In the Bible it says that whoever is vile will get viler, whoever is pure, purer (see Revelation 22:11). Everything is heading toward a climax. In the Old Testament we read, "And afterward, I will pour out my Spirit on all people. Your sons and daughters will prophesy, your old men will dream dreams, your young men will see visions. Even on my servants, both men and women, I will pour out my Spirit in those days" (Joel 2:28–29). We see that happening now. So many young people are being filled with the Holy Spirit, and also many Jews.

So many Christians prayed and fasted during the Six Day War in Israel in 1967. I believe in the blessing of Abraham for people and nations: "I will bless those who bless you, and whoever curses you I will curse" (Gen. 12:3). Nations are also being blessed; the peoples who are prepared to stand up for the Jews can expect a blessing from God. That I, an eighty-year-old, may still do such wonderful work is such an unusual blessing. Very few my age are still able to work like this. I sometimes ask myself if this is the blessing given to me by the Lord because my family and I dedicated our lives to saving Jews, and four of us died. Whoever wants to be ready for the return of the Messiah must be in a right relationship with God and other people. "Everyone who has this hope in him purifies himself, just as he is pure" (1 John 3:3). This is possible because if we surrender to the Messiah, Jesus, He who began a good work in us will carry it on to completion until the day of Christ Jesus (see Philippians 1:6). The Messiah longs for us more than we long for Him. What assurance! Working for Him is not the most important thing, but people are the most important. There are so many Christians who feel united with Israel. We believe in the Old Testament and often understand more of it than the Jews do, precisely because we have the New Testament. There, in the Revelation of John, we read not only about the antichrist but also: "Do not harm the land or the sea or the trees until we put a seal on the foreheads of the servants of our God" (Rev. 7:3). In Revelation 9:4 it says that the locusts will only harm people who do not have the seal of God on their foreheads; and in Revelation 19:20–21 we read how the army of the King of Kings battled against those who received the mark of the beast.

Present-day man needs vision and insight. The Bible clearly reveals God's plan. After the crisis of the battle between Christ and the antichrist comes the wonderful future of the earth, when the Messiah will reign.

"Lord, we pray for the peace of Jerusalem and the salvation of the Jews. Preserve and protect them. They are so often in such great danger. Open the eyes of Your children for the blessing that You give them—You who bless those who bless Abraham and curse those who curse him. Guide us in Your truth, Lord. In Jesus' name. Amen."

Twenty-One

In Training for the Final Battle

Dear Father, in Jesus' name we pray that through this message today, You will allow us to understand better what it means to be prepared for Jesus' return. Amen.

In Philippians 2:9–11 it says, "Therefore God exalted him to the highest place and gave him the name that is above every name, that at the name of Jesus every knee should bow, in heaven and on earth and under the earth, and every tongue confess that Jesus Christ is Lord, to the glory of God the Father."

Yes, that is the final certain victory. It will be extremely important whether you and I then bow before the Lord as our Savior and Redeemer, or as our Judge.

There is a great battle being fought in the invisible realms in the whole world. The battle keeps increasing. Ernst Maning once said, "We have reached an hour in the history of our civilization, which we could call the most serious crisis man has ever experienced." This is not something that only Christians see; the whole world knows that we are living in appalling times. But God's logistics are perfect. *Logistics* is a military word that means, among other things, "provisions." God is a general who knows exactly where and how the battle must be fought and where defense is needed. In the end there will be a tremendous battle.

One of the first conditions for battle is that we have to know our enemy; his strengths and his weaknesses. "Be self-controlled and alert. Your enemy, the devil, prowls around like a roaring lion looking for someone to devour" (1 Peter 5:8).

The children of God around the whole world know that we are in training for the final battle. These people often go through difficult times. It is so wonderful to know that the final battle will reach its climax in the victory that we read about just now in Philippians: every knee shall bow before Jesus. But all those living in the time of the final battle will not be the only ones to take part in it. For us, too, everyday life is a battlefield: the training field. We need the armor of God that we read about in Ephesians 6, not only in the future, but also now. We all have to put that armor on because we are not fighting against flesh and blood, but against the spiritual forces of evil in the heavenly realms.

It is possible for all of us to be more than conquerors now, and that is because we do not need to fight in our own strength, but through total surrender. Paul says, "I know whom I have believed, and am convinced that he is able to guard what I have entrusted to him for that day" (2 Tim. 1:12)—the day of Christ Jesus. If we surrender completely to that strong hand, we will be conquerors.

We ourselves cannot be strong in this battle. We cannot win the final battle. But Jesus is Victor. If we place our weak hand in the strong hand of Him who has all power in heaven and on earth, He will make us more than conquerors. Yes, then we can say, "He will keep you strong to the end, so that you will be blameless on the day of our Lord Jesus Christ" (1 Cor. 1:8). You and I blameless? Yes, that is possible—not in our own strength but through Jesus.

"Oh, Lord Jesus, I thank You that even if I am weak, I can be strong in You. Thank You that Your power is made perfect in our weakness. Lord, listen to whoever now says, 'I cannot do it, but I place my weak hand in Your strong hand'—and You will do it. Hallelujah! What a Savior! Oh Lord Jesus, come quickly and make me prepared. Amen."

Twenty-Two

Preparation

*Thank You, Lord Jesus, that You warned us about these days
shortly before Your return. Thank You for instructing us in Your
Word to be ready. Will You use the words in this message to help
us be more prepared, yes, completely prepared for Your coming?
Prepare me, Lord, prepare me to stand before Your throne. Amen.*

Our whole life is a preparation for eternity; we know that.
But we don't realize it very often. These days, it is much
easier to imagine that Jesus could return at any moment. All the
certainties of daily life have disappeared. It is so marvelous to
have security in Jesus.

The Lord Jesus spoke about His second coming: "As it was
in the days of Noah, so it will be at the coming of the Son of
Man. For in the days before the flood, people were eating and
drinking, marrying and giving in marriage, up to the day Noah
entered the ark; and they knew nothing about what would
happen until the flood came and took them all away. That is

how it will be at the coming of the Son of Man. . . . Therefore keep watch, because you do not know on what day your Lord will come" (Matt. 24:37–39, 42). And in Luke 21:34 it says, "Be careful, or your hearts will be weighed down with dissipation, drunkenness and the anxieties of life, and that day will close on you unexpectedly like a trap." Yes, when Jesus comes it will be like the days of Noah.

I am about to set off on a journey to Israel, Vietnam, and Indonesia. I still listen to the news, play the piano, and enjoy tasty desserts. But my suitcase is packed and I have a passport and travelers' checks in my purse. I am also deciding which vegetables we need to buy today and whether we will need milk. Noah's wife might also have cooked in the small kitchen on the ark the day before the Lord closed the door from the outside. But she didn't forget that there would be a flood and she must have been greatly relieved that her family was prepared for it.

Part of the planning for battle is deciding where it will be fought. For you and me that place is everyday life, our kitchen, school, university, hospital, or business. My father was a watchmaker and he was definitely concerned about providing for our daily needs. But in all of this, he was hidden with Jesus in God.

The Lord Jesus himself said that in John 15—as the vines and the branches are linked together, the one in the other, so must you be in Him and He in you. If we have the assurance that we are in Him, then there is no danger that the day of the Lord will close in upon us like a trap. When Father was taken away to the jail in which he died ten days later, he said to me: "The best is yet to come." The way to be prepared is to surrender to Him.

In 1 Thessalonians 5:23–24 it says, "May God himself, the God of peace, sanctify you through and through. May your whole spirit, soul and body be kept blameless at the coming of our Lord Jesus Christ. The one who calls you is faithful and he will do it."

Just imagine it: you and I, blameless! No, we can't do that; it is only possible if we put our weak hand into the strong hand of the Lord." Being confident of this, that he who began a good work in you will carry it on to completion until the day of Christ Jesus" (Phil. 1:6).

I once asked a businessman if he had surrendered completely to the Lord, and he said: "No, because I am way too busy to do that. I am up to my ears in work." Then I replied, "You are just like a mountain climber who has hired a guide, and he gets to a place where it is very steep and terribly difficult to climb. The guide says: 'Let me help!' but the man says, 'Don't you see how steep it is here, how hard this mountain is to climb? Do you think I have time now for a guide?'"

It is especially when we are up to our ears in work that we need a guide. The Lord Jesus is our guide. We need Him especially when we are overwhelmed with the concerns and hectic pace of everyday life. Surrender to Him. He will make you more than a conqueror, and if you surrender to Him completely, He will hold on to you to the end and nothing, absolutely nothing, can separate us from the love of God in Christ Jesus.

"Thank You, Lord, that You are conqueror and that You want to make us more than conquerors. Lord, listen to those who have read this message, and who say, 'Yes, Lord, I give myself completely to You. I cannot do it, but You can. Lord Jesus, hold me close to Your heart. I want to be with You, hidden with You in God.' It can't be safer than that. Thank You, Lord, that You love us that much. Hallelujah. Amen."

Twenty-Three

Prepared for Jesus' Return

In Luke 21:36 we read, "Be always on the watch, and pray that you may be able to escape all that is about to happen, and that you may be able to stand before the Son of Man."

I am going to tell you something wonderful today. You, yes, you! can be ready, even if Jesus should return today. How can that be? We can read the answer in the Bible. I know very well that many Dutch people have said, "Oh, come on, Johannes de Heer [a well-known Dutch preacher] believed that Jesus would return soon, but he didn't live to see it! Peter said that since the fathers died everything goes on as it has since the beginning of creation. So why should we believe that before our time?"

Look, Jesus said that we have to take note of the signs of the times, and if you reason like that you are a "sign of the times" yourself. Listen to this in 2 Peter 3:3–4: "First of all, you must understand that in the last days scoffers will come, scoffing and following their own evil desires. They will say, 'Where is this "coming" he promised? Ever since our fathers died, everything goes on as it has since the beginning of creation.'" Can you see that you are a sign? A sign that we are in the last days? Because, in that case, you are a scoffer. I am afraid that you are following your own cravings if you talk like that. Of course you don't want to do that, because when we one day stand before the Son of Man, our own cravings will be stumbling blocks to us.

Perhaps you say that you aren't ready yet. You will understand, of course, that Jesus is not going to wait until everyone is ready. He is coming and there will be a time when everyone will bow down before Him, both those who are ready and those who aren't. Then the question will be whether you will bend your knees to your Savior or to your Judge. The Lord Jesus himself warned us about it. He longs for us to be ready, and says: "Be always on the watch, and pray that you may be able to escape all that is about to happen, and that you may be able to stand before the Son of Man" (Luke 21:36).

The clearest sign is that the Jews have returned to their own country. I was in California on the morning that the state of Israel was born (or reborn) on May 15, 1948. My host read it in the morning paper and she ran to the phone. She called her friends and said, "Have you read the paper? The state of Israel has been established. Jesus will come very soon; let's make sure we are ready and that as many others as possible are ready too." That woman saw the event, as it were, from God's perspective, from the perspective of the Bible.

Here are just a few other signs of the times. "Many will go here and there to increase knowledge" (Dan. 12:4). What incredible knowledge we have nowadays. Even if there is a quake on the moon, we know about it here on earth because of the seismograph that we left on the moon. Another sign is that the pure will become purer and the vile become more vile (see

Revelation 22:11). Everything is heading toward a climax. I have never before met such dedicated young Christians as now, who are prepared to live for Jesus and to die if necessary. But I have also never seen, read, or heard so much filth and impurity as now.

But that is enough about the signs of the times. Now we'll see how you can be ready. In Philippians 1:9–11 it says, "And this is my prayer: that your love may abound more and more in knowledge and depth of insight, so that you may be able to discern what is best and may be pure and blameless until the day of Christ, filled with the fruit of righteousness that comes through Jesus Christ—to the glory and praise of God."

Is that possible—such abundant love in your heart and mine? We can never manage it ourselves. No, you and I can't, but the Holy Spirit can. Read about it for yourself in Romans 5:1–11. From verse 5 onward it says, "And hope does not disappoint us, because God has poured out his love into our hearts by the Holy Spirit, whom he has given us. You see, at just the right time, when we were still powerless, Christ died for the ungodly. . . . Since we have now been justified by his blood, how much more shall we be saved from God's wrath through him!"

The Holy Spirit has been given to us. Does the Holy Spirit have you? Then you will be filled. He is prepared to fill you just as light fills a room when you open the curtains. Not a small corner, but all the doors, all the drawers must be open. The Lord Jesus wants to live in your heart and in your life through His Holy Spirit. You can't experience His victory at work, in the kitchen, or in the bedroom, if you only open the door of your living room.

Some people think that complete surrender is possible only for people who work full-time in evangelism, such as missionaries, preachers, and pastors. But everyone can and must be prepared for Jesus' second coming. My father had a watch-maker's shop. He sometimes said, "I am a watchmaker by the grace of God." I worked with him for twenty-five years in the business and I saw and experienced how a person who is first of all a Christian, and then a businessman, lives. Father longed for Jesus' return. All his prayers ended with these words: "And, Father, may the moment soon come when Jesus Christ, Your precious Son, returns on the clouds of heaven."

Yes, everyone can live in full surrender to the Lord; you too! John says, "And now, dear children, continue in him, so that when he appears we may be confident and unashamed before him at his coming" (1 John 2:28). Jesus is knocking on the door of your heart at this very moment. Will you say, "Yes, Lord Jesus, come into my heart"? Then He will come and He will do it. He longs for you, He loves you. He longs for us to be prepared for His return even more than we long for and prepare for it.

In John 15:5 He says, "If a man remains in me and I in him, he will bear much fruit; apart from me you can do nothing." You yourself can't prepare yourself for Jesus' return. But stop compromising. In your heart there is a cross and a throne. If the "self" is on the throne, then Jesus is on the cross. If Jesus is on the throne, then the "self" is on the cross; and He, Jesus, will "keep you strong to the end, so that you will be blameless on the day of our Lord Jesus Christ" (1 Cor. 1:8). Hallelujah, He will do it, He will overcome. He is going to make all things new. Jesus makes us more than conquerors at the new begin-ning, the coming of the kingdom of Peace on earth.

"Lord Jesus, thank You that You will answer the prayers of everyone who says, 'Yes, Lord Jesus, come into my heart, fill me with Your Spirit, prepare me for Your return. Take my life.' Hallelujah, what a wonderful Savior. Amen."

Twenty-Four

Joy in the Darkness

꒚

If it's dark everywhere, you can become so discouraged. You might doubt whether light still exists. But even if you can't see the Lord, He sees you and me. Jesus said, "And surely I am with you always, to the very end of the age" (Matt. 28:20). When it's necessary, He suddenly says, "I'm still here!"

I was in Vietnam, in an airport departure lounge. We had to arrive very early in the morning to book our seats on the military transport planes. The only way to travel in South Vietnam during the war was with soldiers in relatively primitive planes. I was sleepy and tired; it was so very early in the morning. It was sweltering and humid. I was sitting between soldiers in their slovenly uniforms. There was a constant deafening noise of engines as planes took off and landed. In the distance I heard shooting; from time to time you could hear bombs dropping. The radio was playing noisy music. On a notice board I read: "During enemy attacks go immediately to the air raid shelter in this corridor." Everything was so terribly sad; I could have cried.

It suddenly became quiet. All the planes had taken off. Then the music on the radio stopped and a calm voice began to read a morning devotional based on Psalm 51: "Let me hear joy and gladness; . . . create in me a pure heart, O God, and renew a steadfast spirit within me." It was just as if God was saying, "I'm still here!" I sat straight up and listened: "Restore to me the joy of your salvation . . . and sinners will turn back to you . . . a broken and contrite heart, O God, you will not despise." It was just like a very tiny piece of heaven in the middle of hell. I suddenly became very happy. I wasn't at all surprised when, at the end of the devotional, a song was sung to the tune of "Ode to Joy" from Beethoven's Ninth Symphony.

In the afternoon I was in Da Nang, close to the front line. I spoke to the soldiers and told them of the joy that passes all understanding and that you can have that joy in all circumstances, if you will only put your hand in Jesus' strong hand. He creates in you a clean heart and renews a steadfast spirit within you. A broken and contrite heart He does not despise. He says: "Come to me, all you who are weary and burdened, and I will give you rest" (Matt. 11:28). I told them of a very dark point in time on this earth, when Jesus said, "It is finished," and then died on a cross. He had suffered all that was necessary to save us from sin and guilt. That is why we can say: the joy of the Lord will be our strength, whatever may happen. Many soldiers laid their hand in the hand of Jesus, and when they left several of them said, "Till we meet again, maybe not here, but up in heaven." I don't know how many of them are already there.

Let us pray: "Thank You, Lord Jesus, that we know that You are here, today—for us, for the people in Vietnam, Israel, Egypt, yes, everywhere, to the ends of the earth. Thank You that You came into the world as a Light, so that whoever believes in You does not remain in darkness. Make us joyful about that, so that we can be lights in this dark world, wherever You call us to be. Hallelujah. Thank You, Lord Jesus. Amen."

Twenty-Five

Come and See Jesus

The next day Jesus decided to leave for Galilee. Finding Philip, he said to him, "Follow me." Philip, like Andrew and Peter, was from the town of Bethsaida. Philip found Nathanael and told him, "We have found the one Moses wrote about in the Law, and about whom the prophets also wrote—Jesus of Nazareth, the son of Joseph." "Nazareth! Can anything good come from there?" Nathanael asked. "Come and see," said Philip. When Jesus saw Nathanael approaching, he said of him, "Here is a true Israelite, in whom there is nothing false." "How do you know me?" Nathanael asked. Jesus answered, "I saw you while you were still under the fig tree before Philip called you." Then Nathanael declared, "Rabbi, you are the Son of God; you are the King of Israel." Jesus said, "You believe because I told you I saw you under the fig tree. You shall see greater things than that." He then added, "I tell you the truth, you shall see heaven open, and the angels of God ascending and descending on the Son of Man."

—JOHN 1:43–51

C ome and see," said Philip.

Have you ever said that to somebody? Come and see Jesus. Wasn't that marvelous? I believe that the most wonderful thing that can happen to a child of God is to lead someone to Jesus. You then know for sure that you have not lived in vain.

I am so thankful for Acts 1 verse 8; there the Lord Jesus commissioned us to be His witnesses in Jerusalem, Judea, Samaria, and to the ends of the earth. It's no small thing, the task of worldwide evangelism!

But first of all the equipping: He gave us all that we need for the task; "You will receive power when the Holy Spirit comes on you" (Acts 1:8). The Holy Spirit, His power, supplies us with all we need to be disciples ourselves and to disciple others. We can't do it, but He can. That's why it is so very important that we are filled with the Holy Spirit. Full, right up to the very last corner of our lives. It is only possible if the very last corner of our lives is completely surrendered to the Lord Jesus.

If we allow Him to live only in our study or living room, then He can't help and protect us in our kitchen or bedroom. Yes, I know, He sometimes does protect us, even if we don't invite Him to do so. But we can only expect to be more than conquerors everywhere and to be mirrors of His love and joy, if we walk hand in hand with Him through the whole house of our lives from the basement to the attic. Then He not only helps support us, He carries us Himself.

Care is powerful. His strength shows through our weakness. I once spent two months in Vietnam and Indonesia. The boiling hot climate, difficult travel, and all the tragedies I saw (plus those I did not personally witness but heard about) made me ill and I felt my age. Sometimes I felt unable to go on. But there were blessings such as I have seldom experienced. It was the power of the Holy Spirit that did it and that was even more evident because I was unable to carry on in my own strength. I was able to share the great riches of the Gospel everywhere, with soldiers, forest dwellers, and missionaries. I saw that the Lord used me to bring comfort, encouragement, and to prepare people to face death. The people listened not to Corrie ten Boom but to the Lord Jesus who spoke through me by His Holy Spirit.

Would you like the Lord to speak through you today? If you don't know Him yet, then I say as Philip did: Come and see Jesus! He loves you and died for you on the cross. So bring your sins to Him and then let Him in by opening all the doors, from the basement to the attic.

"Lord Jesus, I thank You that You have never sent away a single sinner who came to You for forgiveness. Thank You that You have given us such a wonderful task of being disciples and making others disciples. Lord Jesus, hear the readers who now pray: 'Lord, work through me today with Your conquering love, so that we together, You and I, can invite others to come and see.' Thank You, Lord Jesus. Hallelujah. Amen."

Twenty-Six

A Glorious Future

꒥

"And this gospel of the kingdom will be preached in the whole world as a testimony to all nations, and then the end will come" (Matt. 24:14). When I read this text today, I suddenly realized that we can all work toward hastening Jesus' return.

Do you, too, long for that glorious future, in which the Lord Jesus will make all things new, as it says in Revelation 21:5? When this earth will be covered with the knowledge of the Lord as the waters cover the sea (see Habakkuk 2:14). Just imagine how wonderful it will be when we see Him face-to-face.

Everything is so distressing and uncertain in this world. I love to think of these promises; because it is going to happen, maybe very soon. There is so much comfort for those who are prepared. Read Revelation 21:3–5: "And I heard a loud voice from the throne saying, 'Now the dwelling of God is with men, and he will live with them. They will be his people, and God himself will be with them and be their God. He will wipe every tear from their eyes. There will be no more death or mourning or crying or pain, for the old order of things has passed away.' He who was seated on the throne said, 'I am making everything new!'"

These things are trustworthy and true, just as all the deeply serious incidents these days, in Israel and the countries around it, are truly happening. We are living in apocalyptic days; I mean days about which the last book of the Bible has much to say.

When Paul wrote about the gathering up of believers, he said, "Therefore encourage each other with these words" (1 Thess. 4:18). We need comfort and encouragement these days.

I once worked for a year with Dr. J. Edwin Orr. He is a small Irishman, who as a twenty-year-old travelled all over the world on his bicycle to spread the Gospel. He has worked in 140 countries. He once said, "I believe that God has not set a precise date for Jesus' return, but has established a plan in which a great number of people must hear the Gospel before He returns." If that is the case, and, from our text you can assume it is, then we have a great responsibility.

The person you meet today could be the last. But we should be prepared and willing to witness not just because of that. Every child of God has a task to fulfill: "Therefore go and make disciples of all nations" (Matt. 28:19). The Lord Jesus said this before His ascension. A disciple works on his Master's business. You in your small corner and I in mine. My corner happens to move all over the world; yours may be in your own home, office, or street.

But do our encounters with others produce fruit? A Christian who is never used to lead someone to Christ is unnatural. We have a wonderful task on this planet to be the light of the world and the salt of the earth. Tell someone today that the Lord Jesus carried the sins of the whole world on the cross—for him or for her too. Tell them that He said this with great love and warmth and that He meant it when He said, "Come to me, all you who are weary and burdened, and I will give you rest," and "whoever comes to me I will never drive away" (Matt. 11:28; John 6:37).

"Thank You, Lord Jesus, that You want to use us to show others the way to heaven. Thank You that if we have never found the way ourselves, You invite us to come today. We now pray together, Lord, for the people we will meet today. Will You please prepare their hearts for Your message? Prepare our hearts to be channels of living water. Shine on them, through us, with Your love. There is so much sadness and sorrow in the hearts and lives of most of the people we meet. Thank You that the fruit of the Spirit is love, joy, peace, patience, kindness, goodness, faithfulness, gentleness, and self-control—exactly what we and they need. Hallelujah, thank You, Lord. Amen."

This collection represents the "lost" writings of much-loved author and communicator, Corrie ten Boom.

Reflections of God's Glory

Newly Discovered Meditations
by the Author of *The Hiding Place*

CORRIE TEN BOOM

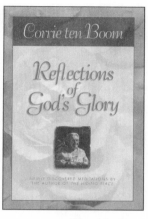

Corrie ten Boom's inspiring story of faith and forgiveness in the face of the Nazi holocaust, set forth in the book and movie *The Hiding Place*, has touched the entire world. And now, the "lost writings" of this veteran saint offer new pearls of insight into the nature of God and the practical implications of faith in our lives.

Translated for the first time into English from the scripts of her Trans World Radio broadcasts in the Netherlands, these twenty-four meditations sparkle with warmth, wisdom, and trust in God. Corrie's stories take us around the world, from her hometown in The Netherlands to the horrors of the Ravensbrück concentration camp, from Japan and New Zealand to Africa and the United States. Whether she is praying for a paralyzed man, taking her worries to God, or forgiving a former captor, her experiences speak to the trials and circumstances of our own lives.

With simple, powerful words, *Reflections of God's Glory* inspires us to consider the lessons of a life lived with integrity before God, and encourages us to trust not in ourselves but in the Author and Finisher of our faith.

Hardcover: 0-310-22541-8

Pick up a copy at your favorite bookstore!

Zondervan

Grand Rapids, Michigan 49530 USA
www.zondervan.com

We want to hear from you. Please send your comments about this book to us in care of the address below. Thank you.

Zondervan

Grand Rapids, Michigan 49530 USA
www.zondervan.com